WALKING IN MY JOY

Also by
Jenifer Lewis

The Mother of Black Hollywood:
A Memoir

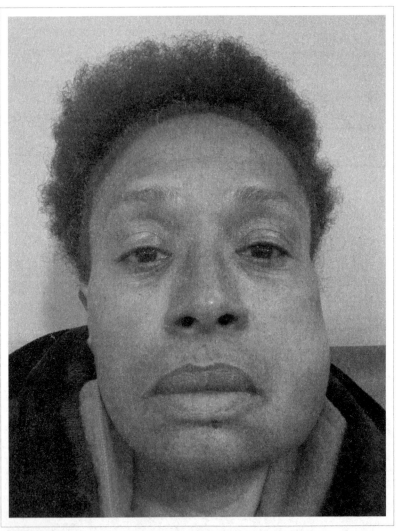

Ain't no shame in my game. This is what too much stress looks like. Y'all come on and take this ride with me. *Courtesy of Jenifer Lewis*

WALKING IN MY JOY

In These Streets

///

JENIFER LEWIS

*with Natalie Guerrero
and
Laurie Petok*

AMISTAD

An Imprint of HarperCollinsPublishers

FIRST HARPERCOLLINS PAPERBACK PUBLISHED IN 2023

Designed by THE COSMIC LION

Library of Congress Cataloging-in-Publication Data is available upon request.

ISBN 978-0-06-307964-9

23 24 25 26 27 LBC 5 4 3 2 1

To Ruby & Hart Campbell

To Kendrick Johnson

And you? When will you begin that long journey into yourself?

—attributed to Rumi

Contents

CONTENTS

WALKING IN MY JOY

IN THESE STREETS

THE BEST PLACE TO GOSSIP on a studio set is while you are in hair and makeup. Even before I open the big white trailer door, there's a certain glow about it, daring me to spill all the tea. On the *black-ish* set, hair and makeup is a sweet, safe space full of warm lights, high director's chairs, and air that smells of glamorous perfumes and too-expensive products. The glam squad, as I like to call them, is always ready to engage in the whispers.

Araxi, my hair stylist, is everyone's favorite. She's a sister. Un-apologetic. Never malicious, but insanely fun to giggle with about whatever absurdity is buzzing on set that day. For whatever rea-son, her sacred spirit and the intimate walls that hold us in that space make people pour out their deepest, darkest secrets. Po' bastids.

On this particular morning in January, more gossip was floating around the set than I'd heard in years. I mean, I had barely closed my eyes before I was inundated by it. I'm not one to complain, and

God knows I love this job, and after eight years we are family, but truth be told, sometimes I wish people would just shut the fuck up. As I slipped my earbuds into my ears, I heard the door slam, *hard*, behind me. Whoever it was would undoubtedly be fired. Didn't they know Araxi could have a hot comb to my head?! Then I was subjected to a high-pitched *"Jenifer Lewis?!"* from a little, sweet production assistant working the morning shift. Now, that fucked me up, because here I am, minding my own business, damn near snoring in the makeup chair, and I still can't catch a break. What in the world could this little girl need? I thought, *Bitch, please oh please, it's 6 a.m. Stop all that gotdamn hollering.*

"Miss Lewis, Kenya Barris needs to see you," she said through her huffs and puffs, having done a fifty-yard dash across the Disney lot.

"Well, tell him I'm finishing up in hair and makeup, baby girl! I got thirty minutes left in this chair."

"No, he wants to *see you see you*. Like, in his *office*. Now."

See me see me? AW, SHIT. In the *office office*? Oooooo. This better be a fucking raise. Did *black-ish* have more green-*ish* for me in these Disney streets? I wrapped one of those bright green Ruby Johnson scarves around my head turban style, put a lime-green helmet on top of it, slipped into my matching green robe, and stepped outside to mount my little red cruiser bike, looking like a combination of Erykah Badu and an insane Margaret Hamilton from *The Wizard of Oz*. Heading over to Kenya's office, the whole time I was thinking, *What the fuuuuck? Why is this nigga making me pedal my ass all the way over to the production offices by the Disney water tower? What in God's name could be so important?*

I finally pulled up to Kenya's office and was ushered right in. He was camouflaged behind his big white desk, spitting words into his cell phone, with gold diamond chains dripping from his neck. Running Hollywood. The king of it now. He signaled for me to have a seat. Then he put one finger in the air and mouthed, "One minute, Jenifer. I'm wrapping."

I surveyed the room and decided on a sofa. I reclined on it like Cleopatra. I looked up at him as if to say, "What up?!" in the most intimidating way. He looked back at me warmly, the only way he ever has, with a smile reserved just for me. Kenya is self-assured. He's smart. Large and in charge. He's the creator of *black-ish*, *grown-ish*, and *mixed-ish*. His show *#BlackAF*, basically broke the internet. He's done more in his years than most do in a lifetime. But listen: Kenya Barris is not my elder, so trust me when I say I did not give a FUCK that he had summoned me. I just kept thinking, *What are you getting ready to do, baby boy, fire me? The whole world loves Jenifer Lewis. My fans will burn this bitch to the ground. Say something! I came from nothing and I've saved all my money, so if I'm about to be fired from* black-ish, *the entirety of Hollywood can kiss my ass.*

He finally hung up the phone. "Jenifer, ABC has called me three times today. They want to offer you your own show. *Old-ish*."

Did this mothaFucka just call me old? And did he just say that a

primetime network television studio wants to give me my own show?
I had dreamt of this moment my entire life. Saw it in my mind's
eye. Wished and worked and waited for so long. I sat up, stunned
and still. The last time I had sat straight up like this was on the
streets of New York City when George C. Wolfe called me himself
to offer me a part opposite Meryl Streep in *Mother Courage and
Her Children.*

Yet for some reason all I could see at that moment were the
faces of Anthony Anderson and Tracee Ellis Ross as they dragged
their asses to Stage 4 at five o'clock in the morning, exhausted but
dedicated to their sixth scene of the day. I mean, these two actors
were in their forties, summoning the energy to do seven scenes a
day. And here I was, in my wisdom years, sitting in front of Kenya
Barris, trying to hide how fat my stomach was. Would I be able to
hold up? It took these mothaFuckas sixty years to make me this
kind of offer. What if I didn't want to be number one on the call
sheet anymore? What if I didn't want to be sitting on a suffocating
sound stage twelve hours a day, bones stiff and body weary from
sleep deprivation? But then again . . . what if I did? It was thrilling
to have somebody offer it to me.

The rumor all over town was that I was stealing the show.
Even the trades printed it: BLACK-ISH'S JENIFER LEWIS IS A SCENE
STEALING GRANDMA. To that, I say, "No shit, bitches." I've sto-
len every scene in every show I've ever done. They should have
thought about that before they hired a living legend.

Ladies and gentlemen, I should pause here and confess that

in my visualizations I have sat for hours in the lotus position on top of the Great Pyramid of Giza and prayed for humility. Instead of "Ohm," I would repeat to myself, "Be humble, be humble, be humble." Shit didn't work, y'all.

After a few moments of silence: "Jenifer. You can't tell anyone. Think about it. But don't tell anyone until we can shape this thing."

You know how it is when you finally get offered what you've always wanted. Be careful what you wish for. I felt a sense of doubt bubble up from deep inside of me. Was this offer too good to be true? My entire life I've dreamt of superstardom. I'm talking about that Michael Jackson–type shit. I've almost tasted it so many times, the A-list. Back in 2002, when they were casting *Chicago*, I remember waiting for the call to play Mama Morton. There was no one in Hollywood more qualified than I was. I had practically grown up on Broadway. Surely I would be first on the list. Guess what? I didn't even get an audition. The phone never rang. Next thing I knew, all the trades were announcing Queen Latifah as Mama Morton. Don't get me wrong. I love me some Tifah. That's my girl. The way she draws an audience in with her warmth is one in a million. Plus, sister girl can saaaaaangg, and she deserves everything she has gotten. I never have been able to conjure up that warmth. *Fuck you, Queen.*

Old-ish might give me a chance to make that name for myself. I sat there, feeling insanely accomplished but, in the same breath, scared to death. Having my own show would surely take my career to another level, but all my senses were telling me to run as far and as fast as I could. Why hadn't they offered this to me in my thirties, forties, or even fifties, when my brain could still memorize lines? I was fried. I was bruised from being overlooked.

I got on my little red bike, clinging on to my excitement, as I headed back to the set. I heard a voice deep inside saying that this was not meant for me. My shoulders dropped and my breath came back into my body. Kenya Barris might have been the king of Hollywood, but I was the queen of my life. His words had validated me, ignited a fire that gave me the big ol' boost I needed to raise the bar for myself. It was time for me to live a fuller life. A life of more meaning. A life that would build me a long-lasting legacy on my own terms, not on Hollywood's. I looked at my reflection in the mirror. Sure, there were wrinkles and crow's-feet staring back at me, but I didn't let it deter me from feeling proud of who I was. I was grateful for my big, bold life. I built that shit. But something made me feel that I was just getting started. Maybe I was on the wrong shuttle about to take off.

In recent years, acting alone wasn't driving me forward anymore. I couldn't imagine pouring more of my time into the dream I had conjured up in my early life. I wanted to dig into a different piece of myself. I wanted to start a new chapter. I wanted something deeper. I wanted more than stardom. I wanted myself, but more well-rounded, not just staying in one lane.

There was a knock at the door, followed by, "They're ready for you, Miss Lewis." I softly pressed a tissue to my eyes, careful not to ruin my makeup. "I'll be right there, baby." I gave myself one last look in the mirror. I didn't know what would be next in my life, but I knew the very next thing I had to do was scene 13, the now-infamous scene of the Ruby wigs. I was ready.

I busted the door wide-open and started on my way, my loud mouth greeted everyone I came across on set, letting them know that Jenifer Lewis was better than ever before and as happy as a lark. I floated down to Stage 4, already standing a bit taller.

As my sound crew wired my microphone through my wig, I was distracted by a talking head on the tiny TV above the teleprompter. There was a chilling image of Donald J. Trump taking his now infamous escalator ride down to the lobby of Trump Tower. *How odd. Why the hell are we all being subjected to looking at this low-life reality TV star?* Then, at that moment the clown announced his bid for the presidency. The world had finally turned upside down. I stood, arms spread out like eagle's wings, making room for the last touches with makeup and hair, as the sound crew buzzed all around me. They had dropped, halting their actions on all sides. I was disarmed. Watching the clown and how seriously he was taking himself made me confused and terrified. This man was the same self-centered, repeatedly bankrupt phony who had purchased a full-page ad in the *New York Times* to hunt down the Central Park Five—now the Exonerated Five. *Oh hell naw.* We the people cannot let this shit happen. This was it, bitches. I was ready to fight. You know how Jenifer Lewis do. This moment was my call to arms. This was the moment I knew who I was completely, at my core. I was determined to fight the oppression in this world. I felt the heart of my power. I was going to be more than Ruby Johnson on *black-ish*, or Aunt Helen on *The Fresh Prince of Bel-Air*, or Jackie Washington in *Jackie's Back!*, or the star of my own TV show, for that matter!

I am Jenifer mothafuckin' Lewis. And I came to slay. Ain't no way I was going from a Black president to an orange one.

Orange Man's candidacy kept me motivated—and dare I say outraged. His words were unleashing the previously undiagnosed malignancy of evil that until then did not have a platform in this country. Things that had been simmering under the surface began to boil up. I think the real deal is that most Americans are angry and have been for some time. I'm not sure they know exactly why, but they do know they believed in the American dream of working hard and they'd have success—not be a heartbeat away from eviction. Most Americans are not living the American dream. They have bills and no savings and believe they have few options. If there was more joy in the world, I don't think anyone would have taken Orange so seriously, but for many he became their voice, vomiting hatred.

I was concerned for the children. Witnessing his actions, our children were learning cruelty over kindness.

Throughout his candidacy, Orange stood on stages, exaggeratedly grabbing at his fingertips, and preached that he was going to build a wall. There needed to be a wall put around him, as woman after woman came forward to accuse him of sexual assault. His words echoed in my head: "You know I'm automatically attracted to beautiful—I just start kissing them. It's like a magnet. Just kiss. I don't even wait. And when you're a star, they let you do it. You can do anything. Grab them by the pussy. You can do anything," he said, later justifying it as locker-room talk.

Being a sexual assault survivor myself, this disgusted me. All the pain I carried with me for so long came pouring out. I begged the universe to keep me steady. His nonchalant predatory behavior worried me. In my nightmares I saw millions of little boys learning the way to be from what Orange Man said and did. And let's not forget about his homophobia. His disdain for Muslims. His hate for Black and brown communities. His greedy little hands, grasping at ways to prey on Middle America, making them believe that he would teleport them out of the hellscape they'd been living in. I couldn't wrap my head around it at first. Like every other coastal elite, I thought, *He'll never win.*

I didn't fully understand the larger-than-life impact of his vicious vocabulary until early 2016, when I landed in Orlando, Florida, to film an episode of *black-ish*. I slipped into the black car assigned to me at the airport and began my doom scroll of the daily headlines on my iPhone while offering niceties to my driver. She was talking my ear off—full of questions and opinions and a thick Southern accent that felt out of place for someone who lived right next to Disney World. Then, out of nowhere, "Well, I don't know Miss Lewis, but Donald Trump sure is gonna make us all rich." I stopped my scrolling. *What did she just say?!* I was frozen, completely unraveled. I chose to stay silent, listening to her go on about how excited she was for a chance at change. It was fascinating, the way she spoke of riches and ownership over the country and a newfound freedom Trump would gift her. The trope of Trumpsters I'd created alongside my peers was proven wrong—it was not just the sick, twisted white men in their basements getting ready to head to the polls and vote Trump into office that November. It was also women and young adults. There were all sorts of people who felt unseen and unheard who were signing off on his hateful rhetoric, ignoring the warning signs, hoping he would make their lives easier. His con was working a little too well for my comfort. I took a big gulp of my water as we pulled onto the set, said nothing more to my driver, opened the door and then slammed it shut.

As I walked to my trailer, in Orlando fucking Florida of all places, I acknowledged that Donald J. Trump had shown us the bones of the nation—a country that has been quietly lusting after crooks for centuries. The only good thing that man ever did was pull back the curtain on the hate the US is fueled on. All these folks living in isolation—isolated by lack of education, isolated by poverty—woke up one morning and decided they were sick and tired of looking at a Black man in the White House. They were ready to "Make America Great Again," whatever that means. As Van Jones said, "the white-lash had begun." There was nowhere to hide anymore. There was an urgency that Trump and his evil kind had running through their veins. I began to imagine the world

Trump might build—full of concentration camps and nuclear bombs and brutally backward men in positions of power. I imagined how our planet would deteriorate from the lack of care from our decision makers who didn't even believe in fucking science. Women and children would be in cages. They would bring out the big guns, the robots—my elegant Smith & Wesson would have no business in the war that would begin with Trump in office.

In response to the madness, I became a woman bent on change. I couldn't be silent anymore. I soon flung into action, taking every chance I got to scream from the rooftops that Donald J. Trump would be the worst thing to happen to the US. I wrote political songs, such as "In These Streets" and "Get Yo Ass Out and Vote." I wrote "Fifty Million of Us." That song wasn't a threat, it was a warning; fifty million of us will march down south and tear down that wall. Those political songs made their way around the world, garnering millions of views on Instagram and Facebook and YouTube, which showed how I began to use my platform with a purpose. My life's work was more in focus than it had ever been before. I knew I had to do anything it took to keep that thing out of the Oval Office. I was interviewed on nearly every television station in the US, asking the public to join me in the resistance, to register to vote, to speak out against the slow burn that would surely be our demise.

I traveled across the country, making my way through these streets with a clear message: NEVER TRUMP. I was inspired by the messages of encouragement that flooded my comments section and followed me on my campaigns. After a rally in New York City, I saw a small Puerto Rican man running toward me with his little boy. He waved me down, screaming, "MISS LEWIS, I ain't ever voted, but 'Get Yo Ass Out and Vote' inspired me. Now, THAT'S a song for the ages. I registered. I voted! Thank you." There was proof that good was being done. I was on a high. I was sure that my work was going to create the change I wanted to see. I was on top of the world.

And then that November it all came tumbling down. This mothaFucka won. My friend DJ, aka Shangela, and I cried that morning like babies and held each other. It was a sad day in the US. Lex Luthor was in the White House. While half the country braced itself for impact, I was ready to go in even harder. Y'all know I'm not one to get knocked down and stay there for too long.

THE BLACK HOUSE

IN THE FALL, A MONTH after the 2016 election, I was invited to the White House to celebrate one of the very last fabulously Black presidential Christmases. Now, I had met the Obamas once before, during Barack's time as a senator, but I hadn't laid eyes on them since they became the most powerful couple on the planet.

I arrived in Washington, DC, and the city was buzzing. I was swept up by it all. In my red-carpet best, ready to make waves at the People's House, with our president in his last term leading the free world. When I pulled up to the gates, my heart sank into my stomach. I'm not often speechless, but at this moment, I could barely get a word out. A Black president in our White House—my soul was exploding.

Ladies and gentlemen, every detail was perfect. The decorations were elegant and posh in the classy way only Michelle could manifest. Everyone in attendance could clearly see that FLOTUS had the grace of a true First Lady. She had done the damn thing.

There were giant gingerbread houses everywhere. I wanted to eat them all, but refrained. The chandeliers hung from the ceiling majestically, dripping with gold and silver ornaments. Next to them stood Douglas fir, noble fir, and white pine trees, all made up with matching decorations. Life-size snowmen lined the corners, and above them twinkle lights hung from mistletoe. My biggest smile came when I caught a glimpse of two enormous stuffed animal statues sculpted as Bo and Sunny, the beloved White House Portuguese water dogs. There was a fireplace in nearly every room, blaring a beautiful heat. The reds were bright. The greens were vibrant. There was no stone unturned. It was clear that everyone and everything inhabiting the White House was made of excellence.

As I bit into a pastry the size of my face, I felt a tap on my left shoulder. It was Michelle's assistant. She looked at me and whispered, "Would you like to see them?" Now, listen, I know I just said I had met them once before, but this time would be different. This was 1600 Pennsylvania Avenue, for God's sake. My jaw dropped. I spit my pastry out, shoved it under Mary Lincoln's rug, and wiped my hands on my dress. You can take the Jenny outta Kinloch, but you can't take the Kinloch outta Jenny. "Yes, of course I do, baby." Little ol' me, finna meet the President of the United States of America. President Barack Obama. Hallelujah. Thank you, Black Jesus.

I was taken into the sprawling East Room with a few other VIPs. It was like being a kid in a candy shop. Now, look, I don't often melt into a little girl, but the Obamas seemed to have that effect on me. I was twirling and whirling and laughing in a high-pitched voice, giddy off the idea that I was moments away from formally meeting the queen Michelle and Barack.

I stood there, frozen like the queen's guard, ready to welcome America's royalty. That's when I heard the *clack, clack, clack* of their shoes coming down that two-hundred-year-old narrow staircase, leading into the room. Time stopped. For a moment I thought that I must be dreaming. *My whole life is made up of moments grand enough for me to pinch myself.* Finally, the Obamas had arrived.

I held my arms out and closed my eyes, hoping they might see me and feel the same overwhelming emotions I was experiencing. *Come to Auntie*, I thought. Instead, they both smiled politely at the room, waved, and made a beeline for a group of unassuming people at the opposite end of the space. Some of them were crying. A few of them were red with emotion. I looked over to Michelle's assistant, and without moving my lips, I whispered, "Well, shit. Who the hell are they?!"

Turns out these unassuming folks were the families of those souls we had lost in the Charleston, South Carolina, church shooting. Nine people had walked into a church to pray in June of 2015 and were murdered by Dylann Roof, a white teenager. The Obamas had their priorities straight. I watched as the First Couple held them. They rocked them. They made them smile. They offered words of kindness and support. They led with their love unintentionally showing us all how to show up.

Their overwhelming compassion and grace inspired me to no

end. There it was again, that familiar calling inside of me to do more. I no longer just wanted to laugh and dance with the Obamas until the sun came up. Well, okay, I did a little bit. But more than that I wanted to act as a leader in the same ways they did. I wanted to pick up the torch. I know, I know, I have no real chance at the presidency (or so you think), but watching them left me determined to show up in the world differently.

The Obamas finished up with the families and then made their way down the line of corporate executives, world leaders, Hollywood stars, and other so-called VIPs. We were all humbled. Equalized, in a way. Their actions showed us who the real VIPs were in the room. I honored that to the fullest degree.

When Barack Obama stopped before me, I let out a silent scream. I morphed into a schoolgirl who could barely speak. When the hell have I ever struggled to find my words?! He tossed his head back, and out came his booming laugh. That innate joy had won him the presidency seven years before. Michelle opened her arms wider than anyone has ever opened their arms to me. They both cried out, "Jenifer Lewis!" I was humbled, they knew my full name, and warmly welcomed me as though we'd known one another our entire lives. A lesson in being well prepped and surrounded by people who pay attention to details. Miranda Priestly style from *The Devil Wears Prada*.

"How have you been, Jenifer?!" Michelle said, looking directly into my eyes. "We're enjoying you so much on *black-ish*. Welcome, honey!" I died a little bit inside.

Then the president himself turned to me. Michelle's man. Boy, was he beautiful. Every Black woman in America has a secret crush on Barack Obama, but every Black woman in America also knows the power of Michelle's swing from the muscles that protrude from her shoulders, so I can't even joke about it. All I'm saying is that Michelle struck gold. And please, Barack's even luckier to have landed Michelle.

The president grabbed my hand (*Please help me, Black Jesus*) and looked at me and let out a big sigh. "Jenifer Lewis," he said in the Obama voice. "Now, you play everyone's mama. And sometimes the mean mama." Then he turned to address the room. "But look at her. She's sweet."

"Sweet" has never been the first word people use to describe me. I melted. "Sweet? Oh, thank you so very much, Mr. President," I said back to him.

I thought, *Well, if I'm so sweet, can I have a little sugar?* At that moment I felt the full force of Michelle's perfectly toned muscles slap me upside the back of the head. Apparently Mrs. Princeton-Harvard can also read minds. Who knew? I'm kidding, y'all!!! No, I'm not.

We were ushered closer to where a band played a mix of pop covers and jazz. The Obamas schmoozed until it was time for the president's speech, which he offered to the room flawlessly. I wish I could tell you what it consisted of, but the truth is, I didn't hear a word he said. The victims' families were front and center, right in his line of sight. I couldn't stop staring at them. The way each family member seemed to be transformed by the grace offered to them there that night was unforgettable. I was witnessing compassion at its height. And I was reminded of the gift it is to make people feel safe and supported through their pain, even if just for a moment.

When the Obamas left, I walked out of the room and down the hallway, taking a moment for myself. The next thing I knew I was flat out on the floor. That's right, I had fainted. Passed out on the historic floors of the gotdamn White House. This is the kind of shit that only happens to me. The entire night my feet were killing me. Pulsing in heels that had cut off my circulation minute by minute. I refused to take those shoes off because I had to be cute. It was Michelle Obama, for Christ's sake! Mrs. Fashion herself. I also failed to mention that one bite of fucking pastry was the only thing I had eaten that night. I guess there's a price to pay for strutting around the White House in eight-inch Louboutins all excited and forgetting to eat.

The medical marines were called immediately. The White House doctor came rushing to my side. I was the belle of the ball, the center of attention. The drama was fitting, really. They gave me some water and Christmas cookies. I politely asked if they had anything better to eat. I mean, this was the gotdamn White House! Ain't y'all got any air-fried chicken wings up in this bitch?! Next thing I know I'm in a wheelchair, being escorted out of the White House. They saluted my ass and said that's enough of you! Ain't nobody got time for all of your shenanigans in these White

House streets. I was the last person out the doors that night. They literally dumped me at the front gate, closed it behind me, and put a chain lock on that bitch to keep me out. "I never got my sugar!!!" I screamed out as I clawed and banged on the gates. I quieted down, quickly imagining a sniper might take me out. I'm kidding!!!!!!! No, I'm not.

———

The next morning, I woke up a new woman. I had twelve hours left in DC to see the sights, and decided on a tour of the new National Museum of African American History and Culture in the heart of the city.

The tour started on the lower level of the museum, which is modeled after the bottom of a slave ship. It was tight and dark and claustrophobic. My ancestors were brought here in unlivable conditions, stuffed in the bottom of a ship wrought with disease. How many of those enslaved jumped out to sea? How many greats did the world lose to the slave trade? An African man could have been the person born to fix climate change, but we wouldn't know because we lost him in the Middle Passage. Slavery was at the expense of the whole world. Everywhere I turned there was another unimaginable atrocity. The instruments they used on Black women with no anesthesia mortified me. I am still to this day plagued by what I saw in that basement.

I rose through the museum and, as it was intended, through the timeline of Black America. I witnessed Jim Crow and the horror of Emmett Till's murder. I witnessed my girl Moms Mabley and the magic of Motown. I witnessed Trayvon Martin. Beyoncé. The triumphs and the terrors that made us who we are were devastating. This trip proved to be one of great transformation. I was on a mission to see and feel my history and where I had come from, but I wasn't prepared for the gruesome sights that illustrated the past and pain of my ancestors.

By the time I got to the top of that museum, I was changed. It was impossible not to be. The museum presented our history as a marathon we'd won, simply because we survived, while managing to transform this country, but to me it seemed a bit more like a relay race that was still in progress.

According to a minority health report compiled by the US Department of Health and Human Services, Black adults in this country are 20 percent more likely to experience mental health issues than the rest of the population. Only 25 percent of those mental health issues are treated or reported. Get a load of that. And most Black people live in poverty. Of course, poverty levels affect mental health status. The suicide rate is on the rise too, especially among Black men and boys. Yeah, we're getting the shit end of the stick. Our minds are a product of our environment. Now, I'm telling you the facts not for us to get down and hopeless about them but instead for us to use them to find a new way. If we can recognize the shit, then maybe we don't have to keep sitting in it.

And while all these stats are true, in the Black community, we still deny them. We still sit around playing our Spades while laughing at and calling our cousins crazy mothaFuckas. I don't know why we do this when we know they need help. We turn our backs to therapy. We don't ask for help when help is the thing we all need. It shouldn't be that hard to speak with someone who is not sitting in the shit but has a distant view of it and can help you see different avenues for getting out of the shit. Trust me, it's a complete release. It's freeing to get to dump all your shit on someone else. Let them deal with it. But if you don't want to talk to somebody professional yet, I'm here. I'll tell you my secrets if you tell me yours.

I realize it's vulnerable and scary, and hard. Say your secrets out loud and you're halfway there. I'm listening.

In this race, which I was reminded we were running by my tour of the National Museum of African American History and Culture, the baton had been passed to me. There was celebration in how far we'd come, but I knew there were so many more fucking mountains to climb. Still so much more work to do. Renewed, I wanted to dedicate my life to running this relay race as hard and as fast as I could. My soul was ablaze with hope.

I left the museum and headed straight to the National Mall. I wandered for a bit and then landed squarely at the Washington Monument. Its grandiosity took my breath away. I adored the way it stood. Larger than life. Omnipotent. Then I stopped at the statue of Martin Luther King Jr., the stone of hope on a mountain of despair. Standing beneath it was grounding. That's what I wanted to become—a stone of hope.

Being bipolar all my life, I'm quite familiar with seeing the world in a way that feels larger than what it is. Grandiosity has been a constant in my life. It has given me my highest highs and lowest lows. Yes, it has worked for me, but mostly it has worked against me. Grandiosity is an exaggerated sense of one's importance, power, knowledge, or identity, even if there is little evidence to support the beliefs. You feel larger than life, superior, and immune to consequences. My grandiosity has sometimes made me feel as though I can save the world all by myself. It was time to go back home and focus on the fight for justice. One step at a time. One song at a time.

THIS THING /

This thing lives on a golf range.

This thing dismisses climate change.

This thing is always in a rage,

Puts children in a cage.

This thing lives in the West Wing.

Believes itself a king.

This thing is a fast food glutton,

Got his finger on the button.

This thing has no reason.

This thing committed treason.

This thing has to be stopped.

How long do we sit in shock?

This thing . . .

DICKTIMIZED

IT WAS A COOL MORNING, and I was driving to LA Fitness to get in my workout. These days I work ferociously on my self-care. I don't mean it the way they tell you to do it in magazines either. I mean it in a way that is self-sustaining, all-encompassing, everlasting, and always on. Y'all know Hollywood is not for play-play. As all entertainers, I have to be fit on all fronts when I'm on camera. Body tight. Spirit aligned and mentally focused enough to weather the exhausting machine that is a sitcom schedule of five days a week, morning until I drop, from now until whenever the network decides it's over. Grueling, but lots of fun.

I arrived at the gym and parked my big-ass white S550 Mercedes as far away from anyone as I could so no one would swing their dumbass door open and scratch it. I entered the gym and proceeded with my forty-five-minute nonstop all-out cardio workout, a few weights, and some stretching. I wiped the sweat from my head. Frustrated that divas have to sweat at all, I fluffed my 'fro as I looked down at my phone, absorbed in the logistics of the day I hadn't yet dealt with. I was stopped in my tracks by a sturdy bump on the shoulder. *That hurt.* Reminding me of the time I was pickpocketed in Venice, it took me a moment to realize I had just walked straight into the finest specimen I had seen on this side of fifty. I smiled, one hand fluffing my 'fro again. He smiled back.

"Hey," he said pointedly, almost as if we knew each other. He took another beat as I caught my breath. "I love your hair."

A middle-aged Black man in LA who loves natural hair? Impossible.

"Really, then let's go get a cup of coffee, nigga!" I shot back.

"Okay," he said sternly.

I, of course, was kidding.

We exchanged a few more niceties. His name was Tony. He told me he was the manager at LA Fitness, and I, well, just told him my name. If he didn't already know who I was, I wasn't about to tell him. We laughed at the few things we had in common— mostly just giggled.

"Whatchu want with me with all these pretty young girls in this gym? And anyway, ain't you into white women like the rest of 'em?" I asked in an attempt to protect myself.

"Not my type," he shot back. "I like a mature woman."

And just like that, I did something celebrities should never do: I gave him my number.

He flashed me another smile. "I'm gonna call you sooner than you think." We walked out of the gym together. I went to my

Mercedes, and surprisingly, he went to his. I blushed a little like a teenage girl before pulling my shit together. I *beep-beep*ed my car open and watched him drive away.

I sat in my car for a moment before starting the engine. I was a little surprised that I had just met a man who made my stomach do a little dance. *Interesting,* I thought before turning my attention to the next thing on my agenda. *Very interesting.* I started my engine, and before Prince's "When Doves Cry" could begin, I was startled by a loud ringing on my cell through the car speakers. It was Tony. *Oh no. It's far too soon. I just gave my number to a desperate-ass man.* Yet again, against my better judgment, I picked up the phone.

"H-hello?" I said, hoping he'd butt-dialed me.

"I'm a man of my word," he said, quickly following up with a coffee proposition. I didn't really have the time to spend on Tony, but I obliged. The call was short and sweet. We hung up and my stomach flipped again.

"Don't do it, Jenny," I said out loud to myself. "You know you can't take another hit."

I hadn't felt this way since I'd broken off my last engagement, to a man named Oliver. Six years prior, I had agreed to marry him. We looked good together on paper. He was a marine war specialist, rough around the edges but not traumatized enough to show his dark side up front. Smart as a whip—a genius, really. The long and short of why I left him was that he turned every positive into a negative. I kept believing, like most of us do, that I could change him. If I was sweet, attentive, and wore sexy underwear, he'd change.

Turns out, you can't soften a mothaFucka who came packaged with far too much abuse.

I sat in the car contemplating my dating history. I had just started to get good at filling up my own cup. Could I even help fill up half of someone else's without diminishing my own? Relationships are challenging. I don't even think I like kissing! Most times I just want them to get on with the sex already. Who's with me? I told myself, *It's just a cup of coffee.*

Tony and I met for coffee at a Starbucks on a Friday afternoon. When I arrived, I saw him seated in the back. I'm not used to sitting in the back of places. You know me: I'm comfortable front and center. I thought it was a little odd to tuck ourselves back there in the corner, but he looked so good, I also thought, *What the hell.* He spotted me and gave me his million-dollar smile. I squinted, trying to see if there were any intentions behind it. He pulled out my chair and talked my ear off about all the things he had accomplished. I didn't say much, which was new for me. As a welcome change of pace, I wanted to let him talk. Allow him to show himself to me. I wanted to listen. A disruption from the usual go, go, go of my life—and my mouth.

Tony was a military man. A Navy SEAL, to be exact. Most of his friends were SEALs too. He told me he missed having people to talk to, but that was the life of a SEAL. I felt my heart melt a little bit. He went on to say how he had graduated from Oxford and met his wife. His parents were no longer with us, and he had one sister, whom he didn't get along with.

When I asked him why in the world someone like him was working as a manager at LA Fitness, he became serious. He looked down. "I don't like to talk about this a lot," he said. "I am repenting for my sins. I am a man of God, and I know it sounds crazy, but I killed so many people as a SEAL. My counselor tells me the only thing that will help me live with myself is to give back. Helping people get stronger is how I survive."

I sat there with my jaw hanging on the floor. I felt compassion for him. He was alone. *How I meet these military guys is beyond me. Give me an Obama type, please, somebody!*

I leaned into the story, enamored and a touch skeptical of the man who was sitting before me. He seemed too perfect. Almost handmade for me. Almost too good to be true. But then again, mostly everything in my life is too good to be true, so why the hell would this be any different?

My relationship with God has sometimes been fraught, but for some reason, at this moment, I was certain that God had sent me a man.

After our moving conversation, Tony and I went our separate ways. On my way home, I shook off the meeting, then quickly turned my attention to what I might wear to receive the upcoming honorary doctorate, for my professional accomplishments as well as my community activism, in front of 11,000 people at Webster University's commencement ceremony. Following, I would be on my way to Seattle, and I pondered what I would say to an audience of 2,130 people at a 5th Avenue Theatre fundraiser. The next stop would be New York City. My mind raced about who would do my makeup for my Career Achievement Award from the American Black Film Festival. I was slammed; who had time for a relationship?

I was truly looking forward to going back to Webster University, from where I graduated while I still lived in Kinloch, Missouri, a small town right out by the St. Louis airport. That was also the city where I first learned the lesson of rolling with the punches. Kinloch's population is three thousand. At one point, it was the largest all-Black, self-governing municipality in the United States. Today, it barely exists. Its residents relocated to make way for an expansion of the airport. Ah, the things this country does to communities of color.

Kinloch was a poverty-stricken community. And yes, there were times when I was hungry as a child.

Kinloch sits just west of Ferguson, Missouri, where, throughout the 1960s, I was warned never to go alone. We were not welcome in Ferguson because it was a white community. But, you see, Ferguson had a movie theater and Kinloch did not. Almost every Saturday afternoon, there I was, a twelve-year-old kid sitting alone in the dark balcony with my seventy-five-cent popcorn, imagining myself starring up there on the screen. I was unaware of the evils of the world. I had a dream and would let nothing interfere with it.

Each season in Kinloch entered like a prima donna. It might

be full of rage and spirit or have an unapologetic tendency to kill you with its kindness. There was something about the unexpected nature of the outside world that intrigued me. One day I'd be speeding my bike through a pile of crunchy red and orange leaves and without warning the next day I'd be snowed in. I'd run outside, bundled up and ready to build a snowman, smearing mud from beneath the ice to make a smile. I'd even find a branch and stick it between his legs like a giant penis when Mama wasn't looking.

It was the seasons in Kinloch that taught me how to pay attention. I knew every pothole on every street. I'd tear the lid off a trash can and sled down the hills with my eyes closed, dodging danger as though I did it for a living. By the time I was thirteen years old, when I'd feel the air and look at the trees, I could correctly predict what the next day would hold. Of course, sometimes I'd be swept off my feet, met with an unimaginable tornado or a hideous humidity that smothered me whole. But for the most part I knew what was coming.

When I moved to California, I thought I had landed in paradise. The seasons here are much less chaotic. The transitions sort of creep up quietly. The seasons ask us to trust, and we do, having faith that we'll continue to wake up to sunny skies.

Ah, seasons. We all experience them internally by going through physical changes. We blossom. Parts of us die. We transform. We go cold.

In 2015, when I first met Tony, I found myself in a particularly sweet season. I was quite frankly proud and in awe of who I had grown into. Y'all know how I roll.

I was on top of the world. Walking in my joy, I loved being alive. I was fifty-eight years old and had just booked *black-ish*. I was a Black woman, middle-aged, healthy, motivated, and as fabulous as ever. I ain't gonna lie to y'all, I was pretty much in love with me. Yeah, I'm aging like everyone else, but y'all know this good Black don't crack. I had recently begun to wear my hair in an Afro again. It was a symbol that screamed, *I LOVE ME!* I see my curly hair as antennas to God. We always fussing with it, but Black hair is powerful. Black hair is the only thing on the planet that defies gravity.

I remember thinking, *I'm doing so good on my own.* The truth is, as a little girl I never envied Cinderella or her fucking slippers. I never saw a husband in my dreams. I never saw a white picket fence. Over the years I had come to believe Jenny Lewis just wasn't meant to be somebody's wife. Ain't no way I was going to have anybody telling me what the fuck to do. But above all, I did not want to get myself into a situation that my alpha ass would be stuck in. I ain't got time in these streets to be compromising for too much shit. Judge me if you will, but I was married to the world. Married to my work and humanitarian causes and all the things that made me feel most like myself. I never found those things with a man.

Then, on the other hand, sometimes in rare moments, climbing into a cold bed alone, a little part inside of me wondered if all my broken engagements and rants about independent woman-hood were a facade. There was a tiny sliver of me that whispered they were. Like leeches, these conflicting thoughts sucked my confidence dry and replaced it with insecurity. I mean, let's get down to it. There's something in all of us that wants to find that happily-ever-after love. That exhale. That comfort of feeling pro-tected at night under the covers with a friend and a lover. Maybe it wasn't my dream to have, but maybe I wanted it more than I could admit. Of course, I regularly quieted that nasty bitch of a voice and kept it moving.

My phone rang. Once again, my thoughts were interrupted by Tony. It had been only fifteen minutes since we'd left each other's side. I was horrified. I wanted to say, "Baby you can't call me this much!" I was too busy, but I felt wanted. I answered the call. Let's be real: it was all kinda sexy.

"So, what'd you think of our first date?" Tony whispered.

"Yeah, you passed the test, nigga. I'm out of town the next few weeks, but I'll catch you when I get home."

"We just met and you're leaving town already?"

Okay now, this mothaFucka might be a little too needy for me. I was a little too busy in these streets for all that. He was adamant that we meet before I left town again. So, I agreed to a second date the following day. I was intentionally going against my gut to prove to myself that I could soften my heart to love, and I secretly loved all the attention.

The next day we met at Whole Foods near the gym for a quick

bite. His desperation was well played. Just self-aware enough to feed my ego. I kept thinking, *Well, hey. Maybe this is a good thing. Maybe this is just the thing I need.* We ate our meals, both full of greens and protein, and I found myself blushing again. I loved how healthy he was, how much time he put into himself. That was important to me. If the relationship was to jell, I didn't particularly want my home to smell like ham hocks and chitlins.

I left that date with a smile on my face. At home I packed for my trip to St. Louis, where it would be my turn to enter like a prima donna.

This nigga called me damn near every day I was gone. Ladies and gentlemen, let me tell you, there is nothing as good for the ego as a persistent man hitting your line daily, whispering sweet nothings in your ear. And in my case, there is also nothing as exhausting. I remember thinking, *Take a step back, bitch! Give me five minutes to miss your ass!*

I had a lot to think about that weekend. I was giving a commencement speech as well as accepting an honorary degree at my alma mater. And while I was home, I wanted to spend every second I could with my family. I rarely got to see them anymore. I love and adore my siblings. They do the good and necessary job of bursting my Hollywood bubble. My head would only get so big before they brought me back down to earth a bit. Whether it was their shushing me as I let every and any swear word come out of my mouth at breakfast or not so gently reminding me that there was no personal chef to make me breakfast, my siblings were sure to let me know that in Kinloch, I would always be little Jenny. Not Jenifer mothaFuckin' Lewis.

Every time I visit St. Louis, I ask my brother Larry to drive me through Kinloch. It's a ghost town now, but it is a bittersweet thing I'm adamant about doing. As we drive through, I blink my eyes and I'm transported back in time. I can see all the sights again. Smell all the scents. Hear the hum of the city: the gambling going on in Mr. Smith's basement, the shouting over music, and the belly laughs as Mr. Johnny slaps his cards down in a mean game of Spades. I could taste Miss Benson's biscuits and Amelia Williams's German chocolate cake and Uncle Dick's chili with oyster crackers.

I sat in the car that day taking it all in. I was finally on my way to the dinner that would honor all the doctorate recipients. The event was taking place at the Chase Park Plaza Hotel, a hotel that before 1950 didn't allow Black people to enter. I closed my eyes and let my tears come, feeling the gravity of the history of Black life. My phone lit up in my purse. Tony again. Needless to say, I let my phone go to voicemail more often than not that weekend.

I floated through the night. It was the achievement of a lifetime to be back where I came from, being acknowledged as the great entertainer I had always dreamt of being. My mind was present, and yet I would have to pull myself away from thinking about Tony. *Was he the right person for me? Was he even worth thinking about in the first place? Should I have picked up the damn phone?*

I was snapped out of my train of thought by a call from my sister Wilatrel. I immediately sensed dread. "Where's Mama?"

"Jenny," Wilatrel said. "She's okay, but come to the emergency room as fast as you can. She just doubled over." Mama had been ill for some time, but I think we all were in denial about the severity of it. I spoke to God: *Don't you dare let anything happen to my mother. Hell no. Not tonight.* I ran four blocks to the ER and there she was. Frail, but pulling through like her tough, resilient self.

Let me take a moment to tell you something about my mama: she was a gangsta. I mean a real OG, y'all. Once she damn near sliced a man's arm off in front of me when I was ten years old. Can't make this shit up. Yep, and I look just like her too. We had a complicated history. There was never any affection, but she sure taught me how to fend for myself. As they say, I got it from my mama.

The next day, I went to Seattle. On the plane, I opened my journal and began to write about what was on my mind. My mother's illness haunted my soul. It was time for me to feel my feelings. Let it out. Then I moved on to Tony.

Tony was different from Oliver, and from the rest of the men I'd been with. He was charming, charismatic, and persistent, to say the very least. Finally, someone on my level.

After I landed back in Los Angeles, Tony was stuck on me like white on rice. It was as though he had been counting down the minutes until I got home. I was extremely busy and distracted, but I always found time for him. To fully let him in meant allowing myself to be vulnerable.

We were sitting at the Cheesecake Factory (I know—what the fuck was I doing at a Cheesecake Factory?!) the first time Tony told me the complete story of his marriage and how it nearly destroyed him. I wanted to be supportive and gave him a puppy eye once or twice to show that I was compassionate to his woes. He was being vulnerable and intimate. He picked up the tab—the least he could do for forcing me to eat spinach dip at a chain restaurant. He offered to walk me to my car. When we got to the parking lot, I fumbled with my keys.

Suddenly, Tony grabbed my waist and pulled me in, and for the first time in a very long time I wanted a man to kiss me. We stood there for a second too long, tension building, before his lips met mine. It was a movie moment. So good, I was waiting for the director to yell, "Cut!" But Tony kept going. Our kiss was full of passion. He moved in exactly the right way. Pressed against me for exactly the right amount of time. Pulled away just in time to leave me wanting more.

"See you soon, Jenifer," he whispered into my ear before turning around and walking away.

And see him soon I did. Just like that, Tony and I were on. He was quick to talk about a future together. He showered me with gifts. He framed my honorary doctorate. He did all the right things at the right times. I wasn't ready to be Mrs. Tony whatever-the-fuck-his-last-name-was, but I certainly wasn't ruling it out of the question anymore either.

The day we first made love was the day everything changed for me. One afternoon we snuck up into the bedroom and purposely ran out of conversation. He took his clothes off and stood there, a statue built by the gods. We made unforgettable love. I was at my best, basking in every inch of his body.

He caressed my head. He passed the test. When we were done, we lay in bed, sheets comfortably between us, and he began to tell me his secrets with tears in his eyes. He was a father, so he never stayed the night. His children were waiting for him at home with the babysitter. I respected that. But it left me waiting and wanting more.

If I was going to do this, well then, I was going to have to be in control. It was time for this man to learn the way I liked to live. And trust me, it had nothing to do with the Cheesecake Factory.

About a week later, I invited Tony to join me and one of my oldest friends, Marc Shaiman, and his husband at Katsuya, a divine sushi restaurant that lives up to my standards. Marc's husband, Lou, had been in the Navy too, so of course I went on and on with my loud mouth, sharing every military detail with them that Tony had shared with me. I was proud of my baby. Tony said barely anything at all. "Go on, tell 'em!" I kept nudging. Tony cleared his throat and continued to stay quiet. Polite, but quiet.

When we got in the car, I got a hostile earful. The Navy SEALs and their stories were not to be shared, I was scolded. This was top-secret information, he said. It's private, he said sternly. I had never seen him like this before. So undone. So raw. It was almost as though there was another person living inside him who was begging to be released. It made me feel a little uncomfortable. Something was off. At this point we'd been together three months. I heard my friends' voices in the back of my head, those friends who wanted me to be happy. "Go on, Jenny, give him a chance!"

The next day Tony announced that he wanted to tell his kids about me. I was thrilled. There was the normalcy I was looking for. There was the validation that this was going to stick. He had this whole plan: take them to Disneyland, tell them about the beautiful woman he'd met, ride off into the sunset together. I, of course, offered to pay. He wouldn't allow it . . . at first.

"Let me." I laughed. "Come on, let me. There is nothing that would make me happier." I pulled out my wallet and handed him One. Thousand. Dollars. He squeezed me tight, gave me a passionate kiss, and walked out my door.

A few days later he returned, letting me know he had told the children about me. "Thank you," he said. "I bought them something nice, but you really didn't have to do all that. They really want to meet you."

For the first time since I met Tony, I was touched by this. He had taken my breath away. I smiled and let a few tears fall down my cheeks.

"Think about it," he said as he walked out the door.

My heart was bursting.

Usually when I have a big decision to make I go hiking. Nature is my partner in life. The trees talk to me, help me know where to go next. Yes, bitch, I'm crazy. But aren't we all? I put my shoes on and essentially ran to the mountain. The whole way up, I asked myself the big questions: *Am I ready to raise two children? Am I ready to let someone into my life permanently?* I sat up on the top of that mountain and sobbed, thanking God for what he had given me: A man. A family. A taste of normal. By the time I was ready to head back home, I decided I was all in. *I'm going to invest in this family.*

Tony brought his children over on a Sunday and I fell in love with them immediately. They burst into my home, thrilled by all my trinkets and the bold colors of all the walls in my house, and ran straight back to the pool. His little boy was eight and his daughter was twelve. They were polished up like little shiny nickels, sitting in their best clothes on my couch and telling me about school and their dreams. The little boy looked just like Tony. He wanted to be in the military too. The girl, as precious as can be, wanted to be a veterinarian and loved on my dog, Butters Lewis. They were as sweet as sugar. Angels sent from heaven. Beautiful little darlings full of innocence. My new family. These kids had the key to my heart.

A week after meeting his children, I began investing in Tony's business. He had developed a new audio engineering technology that he planned to sell to studios to bump the efficiency and excellence of their viewers' audio experience at the movie theater. He never directly asked me for money; I mostly just volunteered it, obsessed with the idea that we were investing in our life together. I promised him one hundred thousand dollars and I paid him in increments, first ten thousand, then twenty, then another. I was fifty thousand dollars shy of the promise when we started talking about all the ways we could get his kids through college. We'd set them up with trust funds. Buy a house together in Pacific Palisades. Live our little American dream.

"I want you to meet my best friend," I word vomited one day. "If we're going to work out, I think you should meet her. It would mean the world to me." I badly wanted my friend Vicky's approval. She had been my manager in the early years of my career, but our friendship went so much deeper than that. Through all my boyfriends and rage cycles and bipolar episodes, Vicky had been there for me. I had told her about the money, the kids, all of it. She was flying into LA the following week looking forward to meeting him. In her words, she wanted to see the godly man I had been sent in action. Tony smiled and nodded his head in agreement. No questions asked.

When Vicky landed, Tony had instructed her driver to take her to the California Science Center, where we waited to view the highly anticipated *Dead Sea Scrolls: The Exhibition*. The Dead Sea Scrolls are considered the most significant archaeological find of the last century and were of particular interest to Vicky; she's a Bible junkie. This was the largest Dead Sea Scrolls exhibition ever mounted outside Israel, featuring more than six hundred ancient artifacts on display, some of which proved the existence of a man named Jesus. Vicky was blown away by how much Tony knew about the scrolls. He was throwing out biblical history like it was his job, wooing her, laughing with her, and making sure she knew he was serious about me. I caught myself blushing like a little girl, proud of the man I had the privilege of presenting.

To my not-so surprise, she loved him. "Well, he's a keeper," I remember her saying. She raved about him for days. Her response confirmed for me that it was me who was off, not him. The minute I had my Vicky's approval, all my reservations went out the window. There's no one in the world I trust more. No one who can sniff out an asshole more than she can. With her nod of approval, I trusted I was in the right hands. Tony and I were taking off.

Right around that time I got a call from my friend Joyce, who asked to stay at my place for a few weeks while she went on some high-level Hollywood auditions. She was in a pickle and needed somewhere to lay her head. I obliged. There is nothing that fills me up more than giving peace of mind to the people around me who need it most. Plus, I was thrilled to show off my Tony to her, hopeful that she would hit it off with him the same way Vicky had.

Tony didn't dazzle Joyce in the same way he had Vicky. They got along just fine, both keeping to themselves, dancing around each other, and silently sparring for my attention. He was there damn near every day on his lunch hour up in my office, working on his business, but always rushing home to his children at night. I had a hunch Joyce resented the time he took away from her, but she never said it out loud.

One afternoon, just before Tony left to pick up the kids, he pushed me into the bedroom. We weren't having much sex lately, but the times we did were divine, so Lord forgive me, I was excited. I noticed he seemed flustered, and his face was pale, like he had seen a ghost.

"Jenifer, I know Joyce is your friend, but I have to tell you something. It's going to be hard to hear."

I let the silence do what it does and looked at him like, *Well, get on with it, nigga. What'd she do?*

"She made a pass at me," he claimed firmly.

I was horrified. It was a shot to the heart. I asked him the details. I was wrapped around his little finger, hanging on to every word as he illustrated the way she bumped him in the kitchen, gave him *that* look, and then quietly asked him to meet her upstairs. I scoffed, trying to convince myself that Joyce would never do that to me. Still, when I saw her around the house the next day, it was far too weird. After all, we had been hoes together in our New York days. I had this creeping doubt in my brain. It wasn't enough to ruin the friendship of someone I love, but it was just enough to think about moving her out of my home. Help her get on her own two feet, you know? Before I had the chance to break the news to her, Joyce announced that she had booked a role on a big TV show and would be finding a place closer to the set in

Santa Monica. She hugged me tight, told me she was happy for me and knew I deserved some privacy with Tony. I kissed her on the cheek and sent her on her way. I watched as she pulled out of the driveway, wondering if she was running away from the truth of what she'd done. I slipped it out of my mind, giving her the benefit of the doubt. Bitch.

The next night I invited a few of my best girlfriends over for one of our famously fun hot tub nights. I put candles out, as I usually did while we spa'd. We couldn't really see one another's faces, which made it even more fun to carry on, laughing about politics, dating, showbiz, and whatever. Everyone was so excited for me. I had a boyfriend. Finally, one that might stick.

As we sat there, bubbling in the tub, my sistah gurls started shouting out their questions in excitement.

"OUUUUU, THIS GUY IS A SEAL!!!?"

"OXFORD, YASS BITCH. YOU BETTA KEEP HIM!"

"OKAY, MAMA, I SEE YOU. YOU READY TO BE A MOM, BITCH?!"

"YOU LOVE KIDS, JENNY! THIS WILL BE GOOD FOR YOU!!!"

"WHERE'S THE RING, NIGGGGGAA!?"

I laughed with them like a teenager and let the beans spill about everything. I told them about how I planned to make these kids happy. I explained how resolved I was about it all, that I was ready, that there was something inside me just telling me to dive into it. I told them about how he had framed my honorary doctorate from Webster University and presented it to me one day, giving me the sweetest solo round of applause I'd ever seen.

"Huh," my friend Brenda said. "I once got sucked into a cult who clapped for us just like that."

I rolled my eyes. *Jealous bitch.*

"Soooo when am I going to lunch with you and Toooony," she asked again in her high-pitched voice.

"Oh, well, right now we just kinda . . . want to be alone," I mumbled, annoyed by her attempt to sabotage my happiness.

Brenda brushed it off and started singing: "JENNNNNYYYYY'S IN LOOOOOOVE, JENNY'S IN LOOOOOOVE." But I later found out she wondered, *When the FUCK did Jenifer start mumbling about anything?*

I wrapped myself in my towel and looked her dead in the eye, still bothered by her demeanor. "Brenda, don't get ahead of yourself," I blurted out. "This nigga could be a con artist for all I know."

The girls went home and Brenda stayed back, firmly planted on my white down-filled couch.

"So, Jenny, you really getting ready to marry this man?"

"Yeah, Bren-Bren. I deserve to be happy," I mumbled again.

She told me she was worried about me. She didn't understand how I had changed my definition of "happiness" to include a man so quickly. "I thought you weren't born to be nobody's wife, Jenny. You've been talking about all that shit for years!" she said, pressing me again. She had a lot of questions—not ones that resembled the lightheartedness of the girls in the tub, but ones that made me second-guess what the hell I was doing. "There's just something here that's not right," she insisted.

I was crushed that one of my best friends couldn't find it in her heart to share in my joy and be happy for me.

"Don't ruin this for me, Brenda," I snapped.

She shut down completely, gathered her belongings, gave me a big hug, and walked out.

The next morning, Tony and I had a photo shoot for his audio business scheduled at my house. We took a break from the photos and walked over to Starbucks hand in hand to grab a coffee. Against my better judgment, I started prodding him with the questions Brenda had left me with the night before: What exactly is our life going to look like? Why did you start your business again? How are you balancing your fitness and start-up gigs? Who are your clients? How will we split parenting responsibilities?

Suddenly, he was angry. It seemed there was an impulsive and extremely irritable madman living inside him and was triggered alive. He snatched his hand from mine, boiling with anger. "Stop with all your questions, Jenifer!"

He went on about how I sounded just like his ex-girlfriends. He said I had begun to display signs of mistrust. He questioned why I didn't believe in him the way he believed in me. He stopped dead in his tracks and told me that he needed my support, not my interrogation. I swallowed the rest of my questions down, regretting my instinct to listen to Brenda's doubts about my relationship. *I have something so good, and here I am sabotaging it.* I let it go quickly, not wanting to ruin our day together. We walked back in silence. My cheeks were hot as I held in my confused rage for the first time since I could remember. I always let my rage out. In a healthy way, of course. Just kidding!

We had just walked in the door and locked it behind us when I suddenly heard a horn blow outside. Nobody honks their horns in Sherman Oaks. It's practically social suicide to disturb the peace like that in our community. Ready to fight for my block, I rushed outside to check who in God's name was beeping. It was Brenda.

Through her car window I could see she was out of breath, red in the face and hyperventilating. She rolled down her window and begged me to hop in the passenger seat. She was shaking uncontrollably. Her entire body was nearly in cardiac arrest. My mother used to shake like this when my father would come in drunk. I pleaded with her to stop. "Brenda," I whispered as I opened the car door, "What is it? Whatever it is, we can get through this. We can fix this! What happened, baby? What did you do?" I asked her to take three breaths. She didn't want to, but she did. The night before, Brenda had gone home, scrounged the internet like a Black Nancy Drew, and discovered all of Tony's darkest secrets.

She opened her laptop. She turned it to face me, and in big bold letters I saw the headline:

CALIFORNIA MAN SENTENCED TO
2 YEARS IN PRISON FOR FRAUD

Directly under it, as clear as day, was a picture of Tony.

Everything in my body stopped cold. I told Brenda to park across the street and wait until I could get this mothaFucka out of my house. Nothing made sense and yet, finally, everything seemed to click. My mind started racing. The next few moments were a blur. I had no time to think. My only objective was to get this sick, phony twist out of my home. Now I was the one who needed to take three breaths, when all the while all I wanted to do was vomit.

I looked through the window to the inside of my house. I had built that house to protect me. The walls were brightly colored. The orchids made a statement. And now, right in the middle of it all, stood an unimaginable, evil stain, Tony. He caught my eye in the window and blew me a kiss. I half smiled at him, not blowing one back, and he tilted his head a bit, rocking back and forth on his heels. He had no idea that I knew.

I ran inside with some story that I had to rush over to Disney for a last-minute table read.

"So sorry, baby. Are you almost done with the photos here?" I asked in a regular voice, hiding my loathe and disgust. "I have to get over to the *black-ish* set right away."

"Yeah, baby, we're done," he said, packing up his things. I walked him down the stairs for the last time ever, promising myself I'd never ever let danger enter again. I was sick that I hadn't seen it sooner. And I was outraged that the same glorious God who had "sent me this man" allowed him to disarm me. Tony got into his car and shot a smile back at me. "I'll see you in the morning, beautiful."

I watched him drive away, holding my breath tight. I thought my knees would give out. I sat there on my front steps.

Oh my god. Oh my god. Oh my god. A fucking con artist. My brain was exploding.

Every call. Every text message. Every time he stared at me in that sick haze I mistook for sweetness. Every sickening lie. The website was fake. I had invested almost $100,000 yet never once saw a piece of audio equipment. Him accusing poor Joyce of treachery. Everybody knows a con artist needs to isolate you from your friends, so he could easily get into your pockets. What the fuck, Jenifer, what were you thinking? This mothaFucka came into my life, into my home, into my bedroom and between my legs. I did not see this shit coming, y'all.

Ladies and gentlemen, on September 11, 2015, I had been DICKTIMIZED. I thought this nigga was playing checkers when he was playing chess. Worse—a sick game of solitaire.

Brenda came inside, and I sat down at my kitchen table, attempting to process everything and take this shit in. Brenda immediately started researching scam artists. He had all the symptoms of a sociopath—antisocial, deceitful, manipulative, hostile, and irritable. That was his regular pattern—to be out of my sight for a few minutes and then start to call me to make sure I couldn't have a moment to seriously think about what was going on. He was a brilliant, masterful manipulator. It made me think of the time I almost broke up with him. We were on the phone talking when I told him that my life was too busy and I didn't have time for a relationship.

After that call, I felt a sigh of relief, like I could breathe as all the tension escaped my body. Then the phone rang, not two minutes later. It was Tony again. In a sweet and charming voice he said, "Baby, did you just break up with me?" His tone was low and sexy. I immediately felt insecure and replied, in a tentative whisper, "I think so." He came back with, "Aww, I'm feeling hurt. I don't want you to leave me." And, regretfully, I didn't run when I had the chance.

The *brrring brrring* of the phone snapped me out of this hideous memory. I was sure it would be him again, playing his sick game. Instead, I answered the phone and it was my sister, Wilatrel, delivering the news that our mother had died. I went down. My knees gave out for real this time. Brenda picked me up off the floor. Driven by my rage and sorrow, Brenda and I went straight to the police station to file charges.

I waited in that nasty-ass shithole for hours, all the while on the phone with my siblings, mourning our mother's death. (I muted my side of the phone so they wouldn't know where I was.) After all that time at the precinct the detective said, "Miss Lewis, I don't think you have a case here because you put the word 'gift' on the check stub." I nearly vomited on his desk when he used the words "romance scam." I'd never known pain like this. I couldn't even cry. I couldn't even cry for my mother; I couldn't even cry for me. A CON ARTIST AND MY MOTHER ALL IN THE SAME BREATH? I found myself in the fetal position trying to soothe myself and my soul. *Will I ever sleep again? How will I recover?*

The day after my mother died, I sat by my pool numb, trying to unravel my senses. *When, where, who, what, but mostly WHY!?! Why didn't I see this mothaFucka coming? Why didn't I smell his rot? Why didn't I taste his poison? Why didn't I hear his sick songs?* I couldn't even tell my sisters and certainly not my brother. He'd fly here and kill that mothaFucka.

Dear GOD!!! And where the fuck was my mama? Help me Mamaaaa!!!!!! YOU BETTER TAKE CARE OF HER, GOD. She'd been sick a long time and we knew she was slipping, but gotdammit I WANT MY MAMA!!!!! I WANT MY MAMA'S ARMS AROUND ME. My chest was bursting with pain. My mother—the gangsta who taught me how to fight—was gone. My tears finally came, but now I couldn't stop them. I kept journaling. *Jenny*, I told myself, *write, baby, and get it out. Breathe gotdammit.* I jumped in the pool, did twenty desperate laps.

I sat there wet, feeling dumb, embarrassed, like a damn fool. I didn't give a fuck about the $50K, this bitch done stole my soul. My entire being, whatever I am, was shattered—broken open and falling into an abyss. This mothaFucka played me like a violin. He researched the fuck out of me. Knew every button and pushed them all . . . *How in the flying fuck exactly did he do that?*

I wasn't paying attention. *Why wasn't I paying attention?* I had nothing left inside of me. I let myself be blinded and now here I sat, drained, depleted, done. I was completely empty from this and the loss of my mother. If I had been paying attention, I would have clocked that bastard. Court records say Tony's been doing this con game since he was fucking fifteen. He's as good at what he does as I am at what I do. This nigga's got a titanium tongue, an addiction, and he'll do it again. He'll destroy other women, and men for that matter.

That's when I decided: OH NO THE FUCK HE WONT!!! I would not keep this a dirty little secret. I wanted to warn everybody. I wanted to make sure they were paying attention. I told the whole world. I contacted every government agency possible. I called the police, the FBI, the IRS, the US Marshal's office, Navy SEALs (the *real* Navy SEALs), and, most important, Social Services. I went on *TMZ*, *Good Morning America*, Instagram, Facebook, YouTube, and Twitter. This was an award-winning episode of *Swindler Tinder*. The police detective told me to call Tony and tell him to stay away from me. He said, "If he shows up call the police." If he laid one foot on my property that would be harassment. Brenda made one last call to him and said, "We're gonna get you, you evil sick fuck." She had him on speaker. I'll never forget the only word he said before she hung up on his hollow ass: "*What*!?!?" He never me called again.

In October, the court denied me a restraining order even though Tony had just gotten out of jail and was still on probation for conning thirteen people out of $4.3 million. The fucking legal system. Once you're in it, doesn't matter what kind of celebrity you are. None of that shit matters. They don't give a fuck.

After we left the courthouse that day, Brenda and I waited

for Tony outside. We hid behind the bushes. Gangsta shit. You should've seen the look on his face when I charged at him. He stood behind his dusty-ass-looking lawyer like a little bitch.

Tony was good at his game, y'all, but just dumb and ignorant enough to keep getting caught. He'd been in and out of jail five or six times. Before Brenda and I stomped off, I screamed at him through gritted teeth, "You used your children, you sick fuck! And that's why I'm going to get your ass! Even if it takes every waking day and night of my life."

I got my vengeful ass back in therapy, knowing I could never process this kind of evil alone. I battled with my therapist, knowing at some point I would have to take responsibility for my part in this nightmare. I had to own up to my delusions of grandeur and my arrogance believing that nothing like this could ever happen to the great Jenifer Lewis. Well it did! And y'all, there were no songs in my soul for a long, long time.

I put a private eye named Jim on his ass. If the courts won't give me justice, fuck 'em. Watch me. Everything in me was screaming "Go get this mothaFucka!" After four years Jim finally got enough evidence to build a case and the FBI got involved. Tony had pretty much gone after three more wealthy women. Jim told me the third woman had seen one of my interviews, but she didn't want to believe what I'd said about Tony because she was deeply in love with him. The day Tony asked her for money she called Jim and basically said, "Fuck love and yes I am ready to wear a wire." I never met this woman, but wherever you are, you're my hero.

Five and a half years later, in the middle of a global pandemic, I was going to have my day in court. I could still feel the weightiness of the institution over Zoom. The judge was going to give him four years, but after I read my victim statement calling Tony a predator and a fraud (and y'all know I performed the shit out of "the truth the whole truth and nothing but" with real tears), the honorable judge Stephen Wilson sentenced Tony aka Dumbass Tony to eight years. The maximum sentence.

One day back in Kinloch, I overheard my mama say to one of my sisters when she'd broken up with her boyfriend, "Oh hush all that crying; a wounded heart will heal, baby. You just gotta give it some time." I'm getting there, Mama. I'm getting there.

/ BEFORE YOU LIE TO US /

Before you lie to us
Remember Rosa Parks sat on that bus
Before you tell your tale
Remember Mandela sat in that jail
Before you cheat and steal
I dare you to Google Emmett Till
Emmett Till
Emmett Till
Before the next dawn
Remember the shoulders you stand on
Remember the shoulders you stand on
Remember the shoulders we stand on

MICKEY MOUSE IS CANCELED

I STARTED OFF 2020 IN the hospital with my second torn rotator cuff. I tore my right rotator cuff many years ago, and I was warned that the left shoulder would inevitably need surgery too. On January 7, I found myself lying in triage, awaiting God's fate. I felt vulnerable and disoriented. This was not where I, the alpha, belonged. I should have been having sex with three men somewhere, but God help me, those days are over. I should have been anywhere instead of here. All of a sudden, I was jolted from my meditative state by the sound of what I thought was a nuclear explosion. It was a hack-cough from an old white man lying next to me with only a thin flimsy curtain between us. He had so much hack coming out of him I was sure that curtain was going to slap me in the face. I took cover by pulling the hospital sheet over my head, praying his phlegm wouldn't catapult onto me.

Hidden under the covers, I heard the nurse say, "Miss Lewis, is everything okay?"

I pointed at The Mucus Man.

She replied, "Oh, is it the sound of the sputum?"

Disoriented from the sedative just given to me, I could have sworn she was offering me some type of fancy ramen noodle. In my stupor, I replied, "Yeah, and can I get some hot sauce with that shit to go?"

My surgery was a success. My sister Jackie came from Kinloch to Los Angeles to nurse me back to health. After a couple of days at home, she came up to my bedroom. My shoulder felt better but I felt completely fatigued. Jackie said, "Jenny your shoulder and you sick?"

"Jackie, I don't feel so good, and I can't even taste the soup you made me. Don't come in here. Just leave today's food at the door. It's probably just a cold, but you should stay away from me."

Jackie understood perfectly. When we were children and one of us was sick, our mother would always separate the one from the other six.

The phone started ringing off the hook 'cause my birthday was coming up and my dear friend Siri Sat Nam Singh was having his annual beginning-of-the-year party. I studied kundalini yoga with Siri for many years when I first arrived in Los Angeles. From the breath of fire to downward dog, we remained good friends both on and off the yoga mat. I chose Siri's party above all because he baked a special cake just for me, a cake of my face. Bingo! That was the selling ticket.

I entered the party fully masked and double robed. I had

always worn a mask when I wasn't feeling well, or if someone else wasn't feeling well, or if I ever rolled up on a mothaFucka and they had funky breath. And Auntie's always in a house robe, y'all, but if I'm wearing two robes, you might want to run for your life.

Ladies and gentlemen, let me pause here and tell you the story of the robes. They are all mostly in vibrant colors and flow dramatically behind me as I prance, sashay, or run around my house, or in the streets, for that matter. I am pointed out sometimes in my neighborhood as the eccentric actress who walks her dog in a robe. Basically, I cocoon in them to contain the massiveness of my charisma. They are comforting on my soft-as-a-baby's-ass skin. My agile body craves the warmth and space to stretch and recline in any and all positions at a moment's notice. A robe protects me and it protects you from me. See, on a happy-go-skippy day, it's a one-robe day. A relaxing day at the pool or sitting by a cozy fire is also a one-robe day. But a two-robe day means I need armor. I have lines to learn, scripts to write, books to edit, animations to record in my master bedroom closet. In other words, this double D cup diva on a double-robe day means "Get the fuck outta here. Mama's got work to do." When I'm wrapped in two robes, my energy is able to flow to get the job done, whatever that might be. So if ya see a red-robin, ruby-red, double-robed diva on her way to Warner Bros., Disney, Universal, or Kinko's, for that matter, PART THE RED SEA, BITCHES.

Back at the party, someone screamed, "Jenifer, sing us a song for your birthday." I said, "Nigga, can't you see I'm in two robes and a mask? I gotta go home and take care of myself. I need all the energy I got to heal my just-turned sixty-four-year-old ass."

I went home and took vitamins C, D, and Z (that's zinc, y'all), ate chicken soup, drank a lot of water, and tried every homeopathic remedy I could find. But nothing was working. I couldn't make it to shoulder rehab sessions 'cause I was too weak and had developed a very nasty cough. I was starting to sound like Mr. Mucus himself, and that's when it hit me. The mothafuckin' Mucus Man gave me this shit.

Eventually, I got better and I was back at work without a care in the world. The only thing that annoyed me was that every time I turned on the news and saw Donald Trump it drove me insane. I was absolutely flabbergasted by the way he moved through life and the torturous way he showed his indifference to others.

Black-ish had become my home, and Lawd was I grateful. It was fabulous to work on the Disney lot. At any given moment there was an amazing food truck full of tacos and pizza. What more could I ask for? I spent hours on the lot.

In March, after working my tail off to complete Ruby Johnson's arc in season 6 (ah, life in its totality), I began to prepare myself for another hiatus trip, this time to Spain, Portugal, Istanbul, Jordan, and Turkey. I had heard casual mention of a disease brewing in China, but I brushed it off. I had three months off, and I wanted to see as much of the world as I could before I got too old. (The next year: the steps at Machu Picchu!) Y'all know I'm a traveling fool and nature freak, so hush. I was overdue for some "me" time.

A few days before my trip, I began to feel a strange, uncomfortable tingling sensation on the right side of my cheek. Of course, I ignored it and kept it moving. I had so much to do before I jetted off to Europe, ain't nobody got time for that. That night I set my back massager on low, placed it gently on my cheek to soothe the pain. I fell asleep with it against my face. When I woke up the next morning, my jaw was the size of a grapefruit. Don't believe me? I have pictures to prove it. Yup, that photo opposite the title page is me.

That's right. God literally slapped me across the face and said, *I don't think so. You ain't going nowhere, little girl.* For days I searched far and wide for a logical answer to my grossly swollen face. I went to the dentist, acupuncturist, orthodontist. I even called a plastic surgeon in case this was some real face-altering shit. I mean, what the FUCK was happening to my perfect, pretty-ass, baby-skin face?!

Even though I didn't feel it was a skin issue per se, I put in a call to Dr. Pearl Grimes, knowing my dear friend would and could refer me to a specialist. She recommended I go to a dentist. When I got to my dentist's office, the expression on Dr. Fugier's French face spoke volumes after he confirmed it was not an abscess. TMJ maybe? The TMJ specialist came into the room and damn near ran back out, checking his professionalism by not voicing his reaction, which was clearly "What the fuck is that on your face? I've never seen anything like it." I left there thinking I needed to try something new. Fuck the Western medical mothaFuckas, I was going Eastern on this. *Somebody help, gotdammit! My face is my money, bitches.* I got into the car, and the first thing I did was put on Rihanna's "Bitch Better Have My Money." I wanted to scream the lyrics with her but couldn't move my face at this point.

I went to see an acupuncturist. She touched my swollen face with such tenderness and care. She said, "Miss Lewis, this is a bacterial infection involving the inner layers of your skin. It specifically affects the derms and subcutaneous fat."

"Fat? Bitch, I just lost six pounds."

She smiled and gently said, "You should have a biopsy. I've never seen it this big in the face area."

Gotdammit, biopsy? Is it cancer??? Not on my face. God, noooooo. I sat in my car and called everyone in Hollywood I knew who'd had work done. It took me two years to get through the list. Just kidding. But it would have.

Finally, by the middle of the month, I drove myself to Cedars-Sinai hospital. There was endless security and high tension in the air. The waiting room was a ghost town—just three of us sitting there, terrified. Everybody in the hospital had on a mask, from the receptionist on up. I had never seen anything like it before. It was something out of a movie, the quiet dread that filled the hallways. It was downright spooky, the gotdamn Twilight Zone.

A sweet Latina nurse rushed over to give me a mask and she immediately recognized me. I'd never been so relieved to be recognized before, even with this tennis ball for a cheek. Something about the recognition made me feel that all was right with the world. But still, I couldn't wait to get upstairs into a private room, at the end of the hall somewhere. I turned off my phone immediately. I didn't want anyone knowing I was in the hospital. I didn't want it in the trades or the headlines or in any group chats with my lovers and family. Y'all know how y'all's gossiping asses be.

"Oh my God," the nurse said. "Let's get you taken care of. What happened to your face?"

I don't know what it is, bitch, I thought, *but you better get it gone or the gay boys in the Jenifer Lewis fan club will burn this mother down.*

They admitted me to the hospital, and I got wheeled up to room, yep, 69. I thought, well, y'all already know. The hospital robe did absolutely nothing for my Coke-bottle figure. The next thing I knew they were taking blood, blood, and more blood.

A few hours later, the doctor came in, looking down at his charts. I asked, "Is it cancer, baby?"

He said, "Oh no, Ms. Lewis, just a little cellulitis. This is an easy fix. We'll take care of it tomorrow morning."

"Well, then I have the evening open. What time do you get off?"

"My intern told me you're quite the comic." He laughed. I didn't.

The next morning, I was wheeled into surgery. There were more needles. IVs. Morphine. Antibiotics, more antibiotics. More morphine. And, honey, when the word got out that "Tina Turner-mama" was up on the eighth floor, if I never knew I was loved out in the world, I knew it then. Lying in that bed with my jaw literally hanging off my face, the staff came to the door with big smiles, anticipating my next joke or, for that matter, insult, or just a good old-fashioned cussing out from Auntie. One sweet little sister girl stuck her head in and whispered, "Ms. Lewis, you want some extra applesauce?" I was on a liquid soft-food diet. It was at this moment—being offered extra applesauce in a plastic cup with a tinfoil top—that made me feel like I was ninety-eight years old, living in the Motion Picture and Television home for veteran actors. And because my jaw was so swollen, I couldn't even scream as loud as I wanted to.

But she got the message when I yelled through gritted teeth, "Hell naw, I don't want you bringin' me no extra fuckin' applesauce! I want you to leave me the fuck alone! What the fuck do I look like? One of those Jim Jones fuckin' followers?! Get that fucking poison away from me! And take that toxic-ass stick of butter y'all call mashed potatoes with you! And while you're at it, take this unfiltered pitcher of water and bring me back a fifth of bourbon, bitch. My mother was a nurse's aide, so you know, I detest the smell of rubbing alcohol. I am begging you to get the fuck out of here! Gon' 'bout your business, little girl, and send one of those cute-ass doctors in here while you're at it!"

Well, that was all they needed—their own personal story of being cussed out by Jenifer Lewis, the way I cussed out Tupac in the movie *Poetic Justice*. I would hear them laughing as they ran down the hall, happily proclaiming, "Yeah, she aiight. She in there cussing everybody out. THAT'S MY GURL! THAT'S MY

AUNTIE!" I would never have yelled at that poor girl if I hadn't been so stoned. I'm lying. Yes, I would. I stayed in that godforsaken room for four days recovering from surgery.

All the while, I heard whispers about something called the coronavirus. How bad it was becoming. How fearful the medical professionals were. There were rumors of a city lockdown. What the fuck does that even mean?! This is the USA, bitches. Surely, we'll fix whatever this shit is in a couple of weeks! I had not turned on the television at all. I wouldn't let a soul utter a word about it. I needed all the positive energy I could muster to heal myself. I might look tough on the outside, but chiiiiil', please, I'm just as scared of uncertainty as the next auntie.

My last day at Cedars-Sinai was one I'll never forget. I was standing in the bathroom, studying my face in the mirror. They did an amazing job, thank God. *Pretty bitch.* Just then I heard a voice at my doorway. It was the fine doctor whose ass I'd been admiring for the past four days.

"You're going home tomorrow, Miss Lewis. Just twenty-four more hours." He turned and walked out. I thought, *Mm tasty.* I'd miss this. Thank God that face thing hadn't stopped my sexual urges. I crawled into my bed with my post-surgery lust.

My thoughts were rudely interrupted by a loud ring on the hospital-room phone from Dr. Pearl Grimes. "How you doin', Jenny?" she said, clearly frazzled.

"Much better, Doctor sistah gurl. I'm going home tomorrow."

"Okay," she said. Before I could respond, she continued: "Listen to me very carefully. I want you to get the fuck up out of that bed and I want you to get the fuck out of Cedars-Sinai right now. People are dropping like flies. War has been declared on the medical community."

I had never heard the world-renowned Dr. Grimes swear before. I mean, this diva wrote the first scientific paper on Botox treatments in African Americans. I'd never witnessed her be anything but steady.

I had heard her clearly. I informed the staff I was leaving. I reached for my phone to call my nephew Darren, my current basement apartment hostage, to come pick me up. Shortly thereafter, a tall nurse appeared in the doorway, wheelchair in tow. She let me know that my nephew could not come upstairs because absolutely no visitors were allowed anywhere in the hospital.

I looked around the room as though these were my last few moments aboard the *Titanic*. As she wheeled me through the halls, the sweet little sistah gurl I had playfully cussed out—well, at least she thought I was playin'—yelled, "Miss Lewis, where you going?! We heard you were leaving tomorrow!"

"I gotta get away from this fucking applesauce," I shouted back.

I had no time to adjust to what I saw around me. The hallways were empty. When I had walked in the doors of Cedars-Sinai a few days earlier, COVID-19 was just a rumor. Now it was in full force. It became clear to me that business was no longer as usual. Nothing could have prepared me for the silence and absence of people around.

As I was carted down the hall, I looked out the windows, searching for signs of life. I then spotted two body bags being wheeled in by hospital workers in hazmat suits. It was right out of the movie *Outbreak*. WTF?!

The next few moments were a fog. The leftover morphine still in my system made everything muddy. In the back seat of the car, I saw that there was no one on the roads. There was only one person on the street. It was some *Outer Limits* shit. As we merged onto the deserted 405, I knew this shit was real. 'Cause, excuse me . . . wasn't this the second-largest city in the mothafuckin' US? I arrived at home both relieved and horrified. Above all, I was numb.

When I woke up the next morning. I picked up my phone for the first time in days. As it powered up, I took a deep breath, bracing myself. The blue light shined on my face. I clicked into my news app. I was sobered by what I read. I cycled through panic, despair, horror. CANCEL EVERYTHING, screamed a headline. There were painted pictures of dead bodies in China. In Italy. In the United States of America. Then, after I sifted through four days of missed text messages, a flurry of calls hit my line. Conversations became long as we shared concerns about COVID and comforted one another. I began calling everyone I loved. At first, everyone was trying to have a traditional phone call, but I would call screaming, "Pick up on FaceTime, FACETIIIIIME!!!!!! I NEED TO SEE YOUR FACE. I NEED TO SEE HOW YOU ARE. I WANT TO SEE YOUR EYEEEES!! I don't care if your hair is in rollers wrapped in a schmatta—show me your eyes, damn it! WE'RE ALL GOING TO DIEEEEEEEE. How long do we have, oh Lord. I may never see you AGAIIIIIIN."

Everybody pretty much told me to calm my extra ass down. Thank God my siblings and friends are adults.

After an hour of trying to figure out how to get off FaceTime, I returned calls from friends in Tel Aviv, Monaco, and Salvador, confirming the globalization of this fucking virus. I learned quickly to Zoom, Zoom, Zoom. Compassion, comfort, and calm were all on the quarantine menu. I had to stop being a scared child and learn the recipe for these soups, which were patience, kindness, safety, and above all a gotdamn sense of humor. Not much was very funny during this time, but trust me when I tell you, laughter is a great life preserver when you feel like the world is drowning.

There I was, yapping away, clinging on to the idea that humanity still existed outside my four walls. (Well, let's be real: I have a lot more than four walls up in this bitch, but that's neither here nor there.) A young Disney executive rang me. She whispered, "Uhm, Miss Lewis. No need to come in to record *Mickey Mouse Funhouse* today." MICKEY MOUSE IS CANCELED? Biiiiitch, when Mickey Mouse is canceled, y'all know some shit's going down. That nigga never sleeps.

My quarantine routine became defined by my pacing. I paced

and paced and paced around my home, alone, stalking my own property like a black jaguar circling a reptile. I would not go outside my gates. The Centers for Disease Control was not yet certain how people could catch COVID.

One morning mid-strut, the gravitas of the situation hit me. Almost in special effects, defying the laws of nature, I began to morph from the undefeatable jaguar into a doe. I was stripped down. Bare. All the medals I had won for being a successful single woman in the world were no longer looking very shiny. I was vulnerable. Humbled. I remembered a story of a woman who had spent seven years in solitary confinement in communist China. She had stayed alive by focusing solely on a spider weaving its web every day and night.

When my phone lit up, it was my only signal that there was still a world out there. My dear friend and congresswoman Maxine Waters rang me.

"Jenifer," she said in her unforgettable voice.

"Maxiiiine," I shouted back, shaking.

"Buckle up," she said. "You know this COVID pandemic isn't going anywhere any time soon."

I stayed calm as I talked to her. The news was playing in the background. After we ended our call, I tuned in again, taking it in differently this time. More grounded in it, less shocked. I hung on the newscasters' every word, paying close attention to how one cough could travel around the globe. It was further evidence of the way we are all connected. I'm telling you, it's as plain as day, folks.

If one of us is sick, we all are. And when you apply that concept to politics and everything else, you get a sense of how much trouble we are in as a world community.

I screamed so loudly I even startled myself. "THE WHOLE WORLD STOPPED ON US!" I sobbed. "Believe this, Jenny. Take this in! This shit is truly happening. It's real, baby," I whispered to myself. I felt empty. Just plain empty. But after fifteen years of therapy, I knew I had no right to collapse. Like Uma Thurman in *Kill Bill*, all I had to do was move my big toe. The hell if this would keep me down.

Breathe, Jenny. Breathe, baby. Jenny, you will not crumble. Nor will you lie down and die. You will keep your balance during this unthinkable shit. Gotdammit, you breathe and get the fuck up.

Like a phoenix rising from the ashes, that's exactly what I did. I got up just like everybody else. We had to. The human spirit is a son of a bitch. Let's keep it moving, y'all.

FUCK FLURONA

SINCE COVID-19 WOULD PREVENT ME from living in these streets, I decided that I would build something grand within the living space of my home. I would take care of myself right there. I spent my time planting more seeds in my garden. I bought a new Pilates machine, and I actually used it! Y'all know we buy that damn exercise equipment and usually never use it. I worked on this book and I journaled my ass off. I was doing things that brought me joy. I was determined to come out stronger on the other side of this nightmare.

As if a miracle, out of the blue, my nephew Jason called. He said that he was worried about Auntie. During our conversation, I realized there was no sense in either of us weathering this storm alone. He agreed and offered to come take care of me. He said, "You're in your sixties now, Aunt Jenny. They're saying that means you're automatically more at risk. We'd be there to shop, disinfect stuff, and make sure you're taking your vitamin cocktails. The boys can help you in the garden, and you know you already love Michiko's cooking." I nodded my head and held back my tears. What a savior. I told him to gather up his gorgeous wife, Michiko, and my four beautiful Blasian grandnephews. Without initially recognizing it, I needed them to come be with me. Given that I had suffered from depression nearly half my life, it was best that I not quarantine alone. And coincidentally, Darren had just moved out and there was a vacancy in my oh-so-very-popular basement.

When they pulled up to the house, I put my hand over my mouth in disbelief at how big the boys had grown, but they were still my "little" sweet babies. Micah was thirteen, growing strong in his early teens, with a smile that could knock your socks off. Benjamin (Benji) was twelve, and standing tall in his own shining light. Isamu (ten) and Elijah (eight), the babies, with their sweet faces and young voices, compelled me to give them all loving nicknames. Micah was Micah-Wicah, Benji was Benben, Isamu was Mu-Mu, and Elijah was Lie-Lie, and only I called him Bonka-Boon. You know how you talk all baby talk when kids come in and are so damn cute. All of them had a sweet innocence. They had been athletes since their time began. They excelled at track and field, and football, and they swam like fish. Oh, and by the way, all of them were straight-A students. I had made it a point to invest in all of my mother's grandchildren's education as best I could.

For the next several months, we gardened together in my backyard. We prepared meals and sat and ate them like a family.

And most important, we laughed and slipped into the simple life. COVID was out there, but it hadn't touched me and my kin. It hadn't yet come up close and personal. None of my kin had fallen. I was fortunate, lucky that we were safe from the disease, as long as we stayed tucked inside the cocoon of joy we had created. My family and I got into the habit of sitting out in the backyard, naming all sorts of trees and birds and the constellations at night, not forgetting my moon in all its phases. We sang "Happy Birthday" to each other on our special days, harmonizing like we had back at First Baptist Church. Other than that, humans were quiet for a change; nature was flourishing.

Having my family around gave me the strength I needed to get out of bed in the morning. They protected me by sanitizing everything that came through the front door—food deliveries, mail, TOILET PAPER! Essential workers were out there delivering everything, and bless them for it. In my home, I was well taken care of. I wanted for nothing. In fact, Jason was so good to me, y'all know I had to put him in my will.

The four boys kept my spirits lifted and a smile on my face. The little ones called me T-Janie, and it sounded like music to my ears.

I told the little boys when they first arrived that the upstairs was my lair and they would have to always ask me before they ever came up. If they ever wanted to step one foot on those stairs, they had better ask first. They had to always wait for the response: "Come on up here, baby."

One day I was upstairs working on my book. But mostly not working on it. I was fretting about the deadline I had missed. *Fuck dem bitches.* Then I heard, "T-Jaaanie," in a boy's sweet singsong voice. I could envision Lie-Lie at the bottom of the stairs, looking back at his brothers, lined up behind him in wait. I acted like I hadn't heard him just so he'd release the melody again.

"T-Jaaanie," a little louder this time. I ignored him again, my smile getting bigger and bigger. The melodious tones of their voices and the special name they had for me made me feel like I was truly somebody. I was T-Janie. I was TJ. I had wanted an EGOT all my life—an Emmy, Grammy, Oscar, and Tony—but there's nothing that can match being seen in the eyes of a child. I now had a Micah, Benji, Isamu, and Elijah. I no longer needed show-business acknowledgment. I was content. I basked in the preciousness of it all.

"T-JAAANIE!" he hollered, using his full lung capacity.

Now, that was more like it! "Y'all come on up!"

Whatever they asked for, the answer was "Yes, yes, baby." Whatever Auntie's boys wanted.

Usually when they wanted to come upstairs it was to show me something they had caught in the backyard. That particular time they had a dead baby possum.

I told them, "Well, if you see the mama, don't mess with her!"

They knew I hated that kind of stuff. They would just giggle at my horror.

Every room in my home has a name. Jason and Michiko were

staying in the guest room called Egypt. All four boys were staying on the bottom floor, the room we affectionately call the Dungeon. I named it that when DJ stayed downstairs, to establish the pecking order. Kinloch is my home-away-from-home room. There's a sitting room named Africa where I often relax and sit by the fire. And of course Butters has his own room in the east wing, simply called Butters.

While my family stayed with me, I was called back to work for *black-ish*. Hollywood was filming some shows as people figured out how to be safe from COVID. You know, stay six feet apart and wear a mask and face shield.

One glorious afternoon, I was riding my little red cruiser around the Disney lot, getting some fresh air and meditating on the beauty of it all. I admired all the foliage of the massive trees, the brightly colored rose bushes, and the spring flowers freshly planted. I have found that when I meditate, it can serve as a calming element.

Later, I was still feeling so peaceful and happy as I drove home, just finishing up a long day on *black-ish*. The family was out practicing football in Manhattan Beach, and I knew the house would be quiet. As my car was turning onto my street, I noticed quite a bit of water. The water was flowing down the street—no, actually it was gushing down the street. *What bitch left their sprinklers on?* And with that thought, I looked and there it stood, Old Faithful in my own front yard as tall as I had seen it in Yellowstone. I hustled up the front steps in a frenzy. I ran from room to room, searching for the source of the geyser, and there it was, the toilet in Egypt. I took a deep breath and stood still. Ladies and gentlemen, Jenifer Lewis in the middle of a crisis doesn't stand still. But I had the meditative energy continuing to influence my spirit, still had the calming smell of the vibrant roses with me, the glory of the mighty ficus trees in my mind's eye, and the smiley crescent moon I had seen off the 101 on my drive home loving on me.

Journal Entry

I refuse to explode. Jenny, you will not scream at the family when they return home.

Jason burst into my bedroom, expecting me to be angry. But I was cool. Instead of screaming I stood there, thankful for bipolar medication and the meditation I'd taken earlier that day. *Breathe, baby.* When I first discovered the leak, I had calmly turned the water valve off that was behind the toilet. I surveyed the damage, then saw clearly the balance on an imagined invoice from some construction company that totaled $698,453,823.69.

Journal Entry

WTFFFFFFFFFFF, NOOOOOOOO!

I told Jason we would talk about it in the morning. "But first, send them all up here and let them tell me what happened. And don't worry," I said. "I'm not planning on doing to them what our mamas would have done to us." He smiled gratefully.

The boys' footsteps were light and slow coming up the stairs. None of their usual sounds of playful laughter could be heard. They stood silent before me. I spoke calmer than I ever had, almost in a whisper, which I knew would scare the shit out of them since they had never heard me be anything but loud. "Tell me, please, do we know what happened?"

Lie-Lie stepped forward, like a little man, and said, "T-Janie, I flushed a sock down in there, T-Janie."

I looked up at the ceiling, thinking, *Help me, Black Jesus!* I need you to recognize, this child, he done gone and threw me a double T-Janie. Case closed.

The following morning, I woke up and got out of bed to see the damage in the daylight. I called to Jason, Michiko, and the boys to come up to see me in the Kinloch room. Barely awake and unmeditated, the calm was gone and I was all storm. I was no longer speaking in a whisper voice. I boldly declared that from now on Jason and Michiko would be exiled from Egypt, everyone was to stay out of Africa, and they would all be in the Dungeon together, until the flooded river in Egypt was repaired.

———

One afternoon, as I sat in my garden surrounded by manifested joy, my little grandnephew ran outside with my cell phone—my key to the outside world. Singer-actress Brandy Norwood was FaceTiming me. She's the OG superstar who coined me as America's Auntie. The first time I met her, truth be told, I knew of

Brandy, but forgive me, I didn't really know her music. Sorry, y'all. I stopped at Aretha. Brandy was a big fan of mine, performing my perfect imitation in every movie I'd ever been in. Basically, she loves her some Auntie Jenifer. Brandy, if you're reading this, you know it's true, gurl!!! You love you some Auntie. Anyway, I went on talking to her as though she were just a normal sistah gurl— adorable, but normal. We became fast friends, and she invited me to her rehearsal. The first time she opened her mouth and let out that voice of hers, I knew she had the It factor. It was undeniable. Her voice is truly the vocal Bible. The more I got to know her, the more I realized that her voice is only the cherry on top. It's her soul that makes her special. I love you, Bran-Bran.

She'd been going up for a role in the next big Hollywood feature film. I started to scream congratulations and do my Jenny Lewis dance, so happy for another one of my kids. Then I noticed tears on her face. She looked terrified, frozen, shaking uncontrollably in that way everyone knows I can't stand.

"I GOT COVID, AUNTIE!" she screamed. I dropped the phone. I saw her funeral in my head—NOOO. The weight of the world planted its roots even more firmly onto my shoulders. At this point in the pandemic nearly a hundred thousand people had already died from the disease. We had not flattened the curve, and every day Los Angeles was seeing more hospitals overrun with patients needing to be intubated and put on ventilators. Thank you, every medical professional who has fought in this war. You each deserve a Medal of Honor and a ten-million-dollar check. I let out a piercing screech. COVID had finally arrived at the front door. It had burst my bubble. In my world, if Brandy got it, no one was safe. Not me. Not you.

I rustled through my refrigerator, and I grabbed a fresh bit of soup and packed it up for Brandy. Jason and Michiko protested. I resisted and walked right out of my house for the first time in months. In the car, I called Brandy back and told her I was on my way. "KEEP YOUR ASS INSIDE, THOUGH, BITCH!" I screamed. I walked up to her front door and dropped off the soup. I sanitized my hands, waved from the window, and walked away. I sorely missed the days when I could just walk inside, hug her up, run a bath, and give her some Emergen-C. Life was different now. We were separate. A great sickness was upon us. This was some *Twilight Zone* horror-story shit. When I returned to the car, Brandy called me in tears, going on about how my act of kindness had changed her. How I could've sent an assistant or not sent anything at all. She expressed how much I meant to her. How my will to heal her was palpable. "I love you, boo," I said back. "No stress, fluids, and lots of rest. You're gonna be fine, baby gurl."

Within a matter of weeks, I heard from some other celebrity friends who had been touched by COVID-19's nasty wrath. My sweet friend, brother, and son DJ Pierce was plagued with it. His mama and his grandmama got it. Tom Hanks had it. Idris Elba. *Jesus Christ.* The list kept growing. We were in the thick of it. This corona bitch had one objective: enter the body and ravage. It did not give a FUCK about age, gender, skin color—Black, white, or orange, for that matter. The phone calls that came in the early days of COVID were catch-up calls, but then they changed.

My dear friend Tom called me from a parking lot at Trader Joe's one early morning. It was six months into the pandemic at this point. People were at their breaking points. "I don't know what to do," I remember him saying. "But I can't drive home. Jenifer, I don't know what's gotten into me. I think it's an anxiety attack. I've never had one. I'm scared, Jenifer. I'm so fucking scared of this virus. I'm quarantining alone. I'm always by myself. I have no one. If I die, will anyone hear me? If I die, I will die alone. No one will know. No one will be there. No one will remember me."

People were at their breaking points.

"I'll be there, baby," I said. I sat with him on the phone for his entire drive from downtown LA to the Valley. We were all tired of being isolated, not knowing the facts about this thing. Tired of being alone. Tired of being tired. We weren't okay. The isolation was suffocating.

It seemed my phone was doubling as a crisis and emergency hotline. Once, it was three in the morning and my phone read, "Funny Ass Diva-G." That meant Kathy Griffin was calling. Now, look, I knew Kathy Griffin, but not well enough for her ass to be calling me at three o'clock in the morning.

"Kathy?" I said.

"Jenifer?" I heard her say quietly. Now, this bitch ain't never said nothing quietly. There was no intellectual wit coming out of her mouth. Her voice was honest and slow. "I think I'm in a little trouble. I took some sleeping pills. I think too many. And I don't want to die."

"Don't move, baby gurl," I said. "I'm on my way."

We both had the understanding that calling an ambulance was out of the question. Aside from the fact that it would be all over the trades, there were no beds at the hospitals. There was nowhere to run to. Ambulances were blaring all throughout the city, rushing in COVID patients. Rolling Kathy Griffin into a hospital at this point would be more of a death sentence than a Hail Mary. This was in my hands.

Kathy had recently finished reading *The Mother of Black Hollywood*. If nothing else, based on my experience with mental health, she knew I would listen and help any way I could. I strapped three masks onto my face. My heart was pounding. I hadn't been inside another human's home in nearly nine months. I had to put my fears of COVID aside. This was Kathy mothafuckin' Griffin, and if I had to kick down her big-ass door, stick my fingers down her throat, and/or slap the living shit out of her, then that's exactly what I was gonna do.

I raced up to her front door. I couldn't get to the top of the steps quick enough. Gotdamn celebrities in these big-ass houses. All up in the hills and shit. I didn't even have to knock. She opened her big-ass door. She looked at me like an innocent child, as pale as a ghost, weighing all of sixty pounds. I hugged her, picking her up from the ground so she would know I wasn't gonna let her fall.

"How many did you take, baby?"

"I don't know," she said.

I held her by her shoulders, looked her dead in her eyes, and said, "How many, bitch?"

"I got most of 'em out," she replied.

"You gotta walk a straight line for me, baby. Prove it. Show me." She did.

After making her drink several glasses of water, I took her upstairs and tucked her in and did something reserved only for my daughter: I kissed her forehead. She fell sweetly asleep. I told her I would sleep on the sofa downstairs, but I never left her bedroom. I never closed my eyes. I watched Kathy Griffin breathe all night long. Nothing was funny. We were both fragile. I sat up straight, lowered my head, and sobbed as quietly as I could. I cried for me and for her. I cried for all of us. We were all in so much trouble. I felt the whole world was falling apart.

Over coffee the next morning, I let it rip (as gently as I could).

"Kathy, you know I love you. I'm glad it was me you called, but, baby, I don't have time for this kind of shit. Everybody knows you've been through hell. But everybody's going through hell right now, in the middle of this pandemic. You don't get to quit, bitch. There are women who have fought great fights and didn't quit. Did Jane Fonda quit? Did Harriet Tubman quit? Did Ruth Bader Ginsburg quit? Nobody dies on my watch. Now, gather yourself, call your shrink, and get your skinny ass into rehab. Hurting your-self ain't gonna help nobody. Summoning my inner Aibileen Clark from *The Help*, I told her, "You is smart. You is kind (well, maybe not kind). You is important. Don't call me for this kinda shit no more. I got four boys at my house I'm supposed to take fishing today. Now I've gotta go."

I looked at her one last time before I left. I had a deep knowl-edge that either she'd be okay or she'd be too scared of my ass to try anything stupid again. I quietly prayed for both.

I raged and screamed my entire drive back from Malibu Can-yon. I rolled the windows down so I wouldn't hurt my own ears. For the first time in a long time, I felt hopeless. So wildly endan-gered. A species succumbing to something so much greater than it is capable of handling. Is this the world now? Is this how we'll live the rest of our days?

I thought back to when I had believed this pandemic might last only two weeks. Back then I had seen such a clear road out. I remembered how I had been expecting Superman and Batman and all those Avengers mothaFuckas to swoop down from wher-ever the hell they were staying and save the day. After Kathy, there were no superheroes in my head anymore. The confidence that one day we would come out of this was gone. I was exhausted and emotionally drained. All that taking-life-for-granted shit went out the window. People were crumbling in their isolation.

Kathy showed me that it wasn't just COVID we had to worry about. We also had to concern ourselves with our mental health.

There was no stability. Sitting at home alone forced us to confront the things our constant society of motion hid us from. We were subjected to looking at ourselves in the mirror. And when we didn't like what we saw, there was nowhere to go. No more running. The stillness had shown us our sickness and made us confront our own personal issues and pain. This disease was weathering us all, seeping into the smallest parts of our brain, releasing our desperation, insecurity, and addiction. We were all compelled to see our demons! You see, there was no escape. There was not even a dark theater to escape to. No big theatrical release. No Marvel movie. Captain America was dead and Lex Luthor was in the White House. And gotdammit, I missed my popcorn and Twizzlers.

During the pandemic, 41.1 percent of people reported symptoms of anxiety and/or depression disorder compared to the 11 percent of reported symptoms in the years before 2020. For essential workers, it was 12 percent more. The effects are real and here to stay if we don't get up and fight back. We have to take responsibility for our own mental health and get the treatment we need. Free hotlines opened up in every state during COVID. And after you save yourself, reach out and help a friend. Strap on your mask and then turn to your neighbor and please help them strap on theirs. We have a mission here together. Come on, y'all!

COVID showed us that if you are sick, then your neighbor is sick. Ladies and gentlemen, allow me to pause. I want everybody to sit up and listen to me right now. My power is your power. Your power is my power. We all breathe the same air and catch the same colds and feel the same feelings. There's no room to fuck around and neglect yourself. There's no space to keep punishing yourself and pushing your true needs aside. We are all fucking one. The more we fill our own cup, the more we fill one another's.

Sometimes I wonder how the world would look if every single one of our cups were overflowing. There would be so much good to go around. So much good health. So much prosperity. So much beautiful life. How 'bout we all answer the call? Start with you. One step at a time, baby. Move your big toe.

Oh, and by the way, wear a mask or it's your ass.

/ WEAR YOUR
MASK OR IT'S
YOUR ASS /

Wear yo mask! Wear yo mask. Or it's yo ass!

Wear yo mask. Or it's yo ass!

Yeah, we're in the resistance

But keep your social distance.

Wear yo mask. Or it's yo ass!

Wash yo hands!

Wear your mask. Or it's yo ass.

Wash yo hands!

Wear your mask. Or it's yo ass.

Don't make me have to ask.

It's not that big of a task.

So wear yo mask. Or it's yo ass.

My girlfriend just flew to France.

I said, "Bitch why take the chance?"

Wear yo mask

Or it's yo ass

Or it's yo ass

Or it's yo ass!

Nobody gets a pass.

DUMBASS NANCY

AS YOU KNOW, I'M A skippy, go-happy, on-the-move kinda woman. For me, there's nothing better than booking a long trip to get away. Sure, there have been times when I've swiped my credit card to take me thousands of miles away in a silly effort to run far from my problems. Of course, I'd always find myself in a foreign country being smacked right in the face with what I tried to leave behind. Now, after all the work I've done, I no longer run, because I've learned over the years that I'll meet myself when I get there. What is it that they say? Wherever you go, there you are.

For this particular excursion, I planned a trip to Bali in 2019. This was to be a trip of triumph.

The day of my trip I was so excited to jet off that I arrived super early to LAX. I was the earliest diva at Tom Bradley International. *Early-ish*. I skated through security, and to my not-so surprise, I had a ton of time to kill. Something you should know about me is that I loathe waiting at the airport. I'm not one of those people who like to sit on my thumbs and stare at the gate. If you are, well, then get help. You need it. Just kidding. No, I'm not. Rather than be bored out of my mind, twiddling my fingers in the VIP lounge, what I do love is people-watching, so I hit the airport streets.

After perusing every aisle of every airport shop and noting my *Essence* magazine cover was nowhere to be found, I got in line for my first and only coffee of the day. A double skim cap. My usual. To my left, I heard a voice I vaguely recognized. I had a split second to decide whether or not I should acknowledge the voice or pretend to keep scrolling on my phone. It's always a gamble.

On this day, I chose slightly annoyed kindness. I looked up from my phone and over my big black sunglasses in the direction of the voice calling my name. *Please, God*, I thought, *let this be an angel*. Though my prayers were not answered, I cackled when my eyes met those of my former longtime pianist Nancy.

Nancy used to be one of my main girls. The OG homie from the metaphorical block. Nancy had played piano for Phyllis Hyman, Chaka Kahn, and well . . . me. All the greats. Nancy stood as straight as a pin. She was long and lean. Her smile was radiant. Her outfit was that of a successful musician—flowy, colorful, intentional. Her hands were calloused and stretched out to greet me. There is more talent in those hands than most people have in their entire body. The bottom line is that she was as fabulous as ever. In fact, the only person more fabulous in the entire airport was, well, you guessed it, me.

"NANCY!!!" I screamed. "YOU CRAZY MOTHAFUCKA, IS

THAT YOU, BITCH!?" Nancy lit up even brighter. We love each other. She rushed toward me, both of us skipping the coffee line.

The last time I had seen Nancy she was in handcuffs. Yeah, y'all, before we take off to Bali, let me take you back to 1986. I was twenty-FINE years old, and Nancy and I were on our way from New York's LaGuardia Airport to a gig in Spring Valley, Nevada, for the *From Billie to Lena* tour. Yeah, ladies and gentlemen, I've performed at pretty much every dive in the US no matter how small or stank. Nancy and I were having a blast. We were thick as thieves and hot messes to go. We had it all. During that period, we were being flown from coast to coast by producers who thought we were the next big thing. Back in those days, we strutted through airports like it was our gotdamn victory lap. Airports were basically mega malls with a little extra security. None of that paranoid shit. None of that take-your-shoes-off-and-put-them-in-a-plastic-bin shit. None of that only three ounces of liquid shit. Bitches could actually meet and greet you at the gate! Back then Nancy and I were so ignorant, the way we carried on in those airport streets, cackling, screaming, dishing the who's who and what's what in Hollywood's music and theater scenes. We would buy nearly an entire airport of souvenirs on our producer's dime. Never got caught for it neither. Ah, youth.

The two of us made our way through LGA and toward the plane with our hundreds of airport souvenirs. We were stuffed into that loading bridge, and before the airplane door closed behind us, Nancy made a joke I found particularly funny. I'm always surprised when people can make me belly laugh. That's usually my job. It's a welcome turning of the tables. Through happy tears, I slapped Nancy and said something to the effect of, "Swear to God, I'm gonna kill you if you don't shut the fuck up!"

Nancy slapped me right back as we walked onto the plane, looked the stewardess dead in the eye, and, with huffs and puffs of hysteria, said five words that changed our trip (and our relationship) forever.

"Careful. She's got a gun."

Dumbass Nancy The Piano Player. That's what we'll be calling her from here on out. I mean, what the fuck? Everyone knows rule number one is never scream "Fire!" in a packed movie theater. The flight attendant's face dropped immediately. She looked at me, tilted her head, and pressed her lips together. I acted like *I ain't seen nothing*, laughed, and looked at her. "I'm innocent," I said, putting my hands up. She let out an insincere chuckle. I slapped Dumbass Nancy The Piano Player one more time. This time I meant it.

Dumbass Nancy The Piano Player and I made our way down the aisle to the last row. Per usual I would be taking the window seat and Dumbass Nancy The Piano Player would be in the aisle seat, all the while praying no one would sit in the middle. We were at the midsection of the plane when I eyed a sexy-ass passenger making his way to our row in the middle seat. Not unhappy about sitting next to this fine-ass neighbor, I asked him to help me get my bag in the overhead compartment. Y'all know it wasn't even heavy, sneaky bitch. I slipped into my seat, put my eye mask on, and settled in.

About ten minutes later, when I hadn't heard a thing from the captain, I pulled my eye mask up. The plane hadn't moved a gotdamn inch, and the stewardesses had fallen silent. Not even a peep for the classic in-case-of-an-emergency bullshit speech. Those speeches are so worthless. We all know if there's an emergency on this plane there ain't a gotdamn thing we can do to save ourselves.

My inner child was screaming silently inside my cute, young-ass body. You see, I'm the baby of my family. When I didn't get what I wanted as a child, I just threw myself on the floor and cried. But I wasn't about to get on this nasty-ass floor. So I grumbled, "I want to go to Spring Valley." I'm ready to go y'all, what the fuck?

I was side-eyed by my middle-seat muscle man. It was as if he'd heard my inner scream. Telepathy. He gave me another side-eye and pointed. For just a split second . . . I saw a SWAT team approaching the plane, stealth and tactical in their formation. They were strategically on the hunt. What in God's name was going on? This was some shit right out of the movie *Platoon*. The stewardess stood up as the back door of the plane violently opened, and the entire SWAT team boarded the plane. SWAT stopped at my seat.

"Put your hands up!" they yelled at me. "Put your hands *up*!" they yelled again. "Come with us, Miss Lewis."

"Okay," I said as I pointed to Dumbass Nancy The Piano Player. "But she's the one who said it," I blurted out.

Before I got through my sentence, they grabbed the bitch. Look, I ain't no snitch, but I'm not going down alone either. We were paraded down the aisles like two-bit criminals covered in shit. We were stared down in silence by each and every passenger. It was a disgraceful, sexless walk of shame. Damn that Dumbass Nancy The Piano Player!!!!

Off the plane, they asked both Dumbass Nancy The Piano Player and me to stand against the wall in the airport Jetway and to spread-eagle. I was thoroughly searched. It didn't hurt that the cop padding me down was so handsome. I was like, "Damn baby. A little more to the left, why don't you?" Sorry y'all, these were my sex addiction days.

When the officer was done with me, he told me I was free to go and gave me his number. I'm kidding. No, I'm not. At the same time he let me go free, he told me that he was prepared to take Dumbass Nancy The Piano Player down to the precinct. In one fell swoop, he cuffed her. A piece of me knew that's what she deserved. I was pissed. It was the first time I had an encounter with the police. This bitch-getting-arrested shit was nowhere near cute.

Y'all know I ain't no asshole and I was starting to feel sorry for Dumbass Nancy. Like a lost child, I innocently asked the officer, "What am I suppose to do now?" The officer said, "Well, it's against the law for you to ride with her, but you can get in the other patrol car and ride with them." I arrived at that smelly-ass precinct and ran to a phone booth.

Back in the '80s, when I didn't know what to do, I called my agent, Jonathan. He knew I was a needy bitch, and there was always something going wrong when I was out on the road. Before he could even say hello I started screaming. "JONATHAN! DUMBASS NANCY THE PIANO PLAYER IS IN JAIL! SHE DONE FUCKED UP THE MONEY AND AIN'T NONE OF US GONNA BE PAID NOW! WHAT SHOULD I DO?!" There was a long silence, and then I heard him whisper, "Is this one of your jokes, Jenifer?" I slammed down the phone, hanging up on him. *Gotdammit, Jonathan! Useless MothaFucka.*

With Dumbass Nancy The Piano Player still behind bars, I left the precinct knowing she'd be released in the morning. I later heard she got 500 hours of community service. I had not seen her again until this very moment, in 2019, at LAX.

I opened my arms wide. "Come here, Dumbass Nancy," I said. She threw her head back, laughing, and before we went our separate ways, she gave me a tight bear hug. She was still as crazy as a road lizard. But doing well.

I boarded my plane to Bali, no SWAT team in sight, and I settled into my first-class seat. I was prepared for a trip of a lifetime. I slipped my eye mask on my face, and counted backward from 100. I fell into the deepest slumber, and when I woke up, behold! I was in Bali!

This trip to Bali would be all about me. *Me, me, me, me, me, me, me, me* (to be sung in musical scale).

The suite I was staying in was beyond words. Lavish. Built for a queen like me. I was in another particularly sweet season of my life. The goal of my trip to Bali was to begin writing this book you're reading and align myself with the next chapter of my life. I might as well have taped a sign to my door that read NO ASS-HOLES ALLOWED. On that trip, I booked myself ten massages over eleven days. Kidding. No, I'm not!

I slipped into my swimsuit and stared at myself in the mirror. Go on, Jenny! You still cute. I stepped out on to my balcony as I smeared and slathered sun lotion all over my body. I allowed the balmy Bali sun to kiss and caress my soft newborn baby skin. Picture it. Come on, you know you want to. Who needs a man when you have Bain de Soleil?

Just as I was basking in the glory of myself, there was a rude knock on the door. I froze. Hoping the human interrupting my orgasmic moment would back away and leave me the hell alone. They didn't. They just kept at their banging. There were three more knocks before I swung the door open, ready to kill. What the fuck?! It was Keisha. Keisha from fuckin *black-ish*!

She was wearing a bright pink onesie, a floppy hat, and giant set of jewel-studded sunglasses. She was gripping a mimosa between those perfectly manicured fingers so tightly that I thought the glass might break.

This version of Keisha was different than the Keisha I knew on set. She was usually standing pointing her finger and telling all the cast and crew what to do, where to go, and how to be. A bad mama jama if I had ever seen one. She was a girl after my own heart.

A few weeks before our Bali bump-in (*Please, who am I kidding? This was not a bump-in. This bitch had stalked me halfway across the globe!*), I had told Keisha all about my trip. Through shaky laughter, she swore that she'd meet me here. I distinctly remember looking straight at her and saying, "Please don't." The poor baby couldn't afford this, not to mention this trip was supposed to be a solo one. Clearly Keisha hadn't understood the assignment. The bitch took three cheap flights by way of Taiwan, Manila, and Malaysia to get to me. And not necessarily in that order. I think there was a prop plane from Borneo somewhere in there too. Keisha had literally manifested herself, compelled and propelled herself into crashing my vacation. Pathetic.

Okay, let's be real: I was overjoyed.

"I divorced Todd!" Keisha shrieked, pushing her way into my room, drunk as a gotdamn skunk. "I divorced him! I d-i-v-o-r-c-e-d Todd!"

The next few moments were a shit show. Entertaining, but a shit show. Keisha was crying. She was laughing. She was quiet. She was banging on the walls. Falling on the floor. Jumping for joy. There was something familiar to me about Keisha's chaos. The roller-coaster ride that relationships take us on is fucking absurd. I had felt that sharp pang of grief and relief more than one time in my life. The truth is, heartbreak looks like all sorts of things when you really live it out loud. It can be big or small. It can be full of hurt and it can be full of happiness. It can be full of rage. It can be characterized in a morning cup of coffee or manifest itself as twelve orgies in one day. I'll let you guess the route my heartbreaks have taken. Let's just say, wild ride, y'all.

When all the clamoring was done, Keisha looked at me again and curled up in a ball on my bed.

"I divorced Todd, Jen," she repeated. "And now I don't know what to do. So I came to Bali."

If that ain't some *Eat Pray Love* shiiiiiiiit, then I don't know what is.

When the sobbing died down, I cradled her head and rocked her. I had one thought in my head: This bitch was not sleeping with me in my luxurious bed. Fuck that. Over her shoulder I reached for the rotary phone and called housekeeping to prepare her a cot. After I picked Keisha up off my bed like a baby, we sauntered down on to breakfast and ordered the entire menu while she recounted the dreadful and sometimes delightful parts of her fifteen-year marriage to Todd. Keisha kept saying how guilty she felt for having quit her marriage. I reminded her boldly that quitting was the gift that gave herself her life back.

"You didn't quit," I told her. "You withdrew from the bullshit. You resigned from an orchestra that no longer rehearsed. They're just feelings, baby, and feelings have never killed anybody. The memories will never go away. But I promise you that the pain will dissipate with time. You've just gotta hold on like everybody else. Get yourself some good books on divorcing. You ain't the only bitch on Earth with an ex-husband."

Keisha and I spent the next four days as gluttons. We consumed everything we wanted, exactly at the moment we wanted it. Tequila in the morning, coffee at night, donuts midday, the pool boy every moment in between. I'm kidding!!!! No, I'm not. Though there is always a small part of being alone that can feel lonely, this trip was one big giant celebration of learning how to love being alone. The world was all ours.

When Keisha left, I was a little sad, but my wallet sure was happy. Jesus Christ, Keisha. LOBSTER???? You eat like a cow!!!

Alone and content, I was reveling in the silence. The rest of the trip was an adventurous blur. During my trip, I was driven to Benoa, where I boarded the *Seabourn Encore* cruise ship to make my way around Indonesia. The cruise director himself escorted me to my room—*mmmm*, tasty.

First stop, Komodo island. When we arrived, I felt like Forrest Gump in 'Nam. There was an anticipation in waiting for those dragons to appear. Hoping they didn't slither the wrong way when we saw them with their big-ass serrated teeth. That's a poetic way of saying I was shitting myself.

At the first Komodo dragon sighting, my heartbeat stopped. I was catapulted back in time, watching a big prehistoric motha-Fucka with short-ass little legs and those sharp-ass teeth breathing calmly five feet away knowing the venom could kill me. My tour guide observed the splendor of the animal, then looked at me and winked.

The next trip was to Celukan Bawang, located on the northern coast of Bali. The poverty I witnessed was stifling, and yet the faces that made up these islands were ageless. Their eyes were bright, and their smiles were glorious. I might not have been in Kinloch, Missouri, or Los Angeles, California, but here, in this place, I was being held. The arms that covered me were caring. It was the bells, the drums, the gongs that cuddled me at night. Everything was so full of life.

Next was Gitgit Waterfall, also in the north of the island. When we arrived at the waterfall, there was a sign that read, EN- TRANCE TICKET. RP. 20.000. HA! Bitch, I ain't giving nobody no 20,000 anything to "git" in no Gitgit Waterfall. Git it?

As my muscular guide machete-hacked his way through the thick brush, he explained that this was the VIP secret passage behind the falls. All I could think was, *Fuck VIP, nigga. These mos- quitoes are tearing my ass up! I'm pretty much ready to "git" the fuck out of Gitgit!*

We then stopped off to dip in the holy waters of Goa Rang Reng. There was a strong waterfall pouring out the side of the dragon-shaped landscape inside the earth. Bamboo surrounded ev- erything in all its glory. The water was green. *Now, Jenny, don't get in this dirty-ass water with all these other people. You know this shit ain't nowhere near holy.* I looked around for a moment, apprehensive. Everyone there alongside me was looking at their partner. I was relishing in the moment. I was loving being alone. I took one long deep breath and leapt into the water. That's right, I took the dip.

Ladies and gentlemen, I am grateful for the company of myself. A party of one taking on this great adventure called life. When I was younger, I dreamt of freedom. I dreamt of the ability to sing any song I want to sing whenever I want to sing it, however loud. I'm married to me. Married to nature. Married to the world. Whatever summers I have left to savor in are mine, gotdammit.

So I'll say to you what I say to myself:

Do not feel lonely. The entire universe is inside you.

—attributed to Rumi

/ WE'RE GOING
TO BE
ALL RIGHT /

One time, one nation, one people.
We're gonna be all right if we stand as the people.
We're gonna be all right if we trust we're the people.
We're gonna be all right if we rise, rise.
We're gonna be all right if we trust we're the people.
We're gonna be all right if we rise
As one people.

AGE OF INNOCENCE

EVERYONE ON PLANET EARTH HAS a favorite cousin. Well, at least every Black person on planet Earth does. Oh, you know, the one that gets drunk, jumps up, and slams a card on the table when playing Spades. The one you run toward and not away from at the family cookout. The one fool always borrowing twenty dollars. The one who has promised to be with you from diapers to death. The one who holds all your secrets and knows everybody you slept with and would drag a dead body down the road with you. They're part cousin, part sibling, part soulmate. For me, that cousin was my Ronnie.

When I was about six years old, Ronnie tried to teach me how to play with dolls. I was older than him, and he couldn't call me just by my first name. We had manners back in those days. That's why until this day I can't curse around kids and old people. Oh, maybe I do now, with the old people. I'm sixty-five. I can get away with anything. Fuck 'em.

Anyway, Ronnie would say, "Aunt Jenny, hang her ponytail off to the left so it won't get in the way of the ruffles on her blouse. You gotta straighten her legs real good to get the pants on. Go get her red high heels. She can't be walking around barefeeted." We'd sit together for hours in his room, playing with dolls and dreaming about our futures. And—let's be real—hiding from our sisters and brothers and mamas and daddies because our spirits were too big for 'em.

Ronnie's dream was to be a great hair stylist in Hollywood. And we know mine—I'm living it!

This wasn't my thing, playing with dolls, but I always enjoyed our time together. My ass was regularly challenging him to go outside and roll around all up in the dirt, rake some leaves from Miss Sally's oak tree and jump in the pile and make mud pies and shit. But Ronnie rarely budged. He was always up in that room, grooming his little Barbie dolls. Braiding their hair and then putting them under the old bonnet hair dryers. He had a collection like I'd never seen before. He took great care of his dolls. Using his creativity, he would make the dolls earrings with anything he could find, such as staples and screws. He'd use a washer to make a bracelet. He'd pick flowers from outside and place them in the doll's hair like Billie Holiday. We didn't have any gardenias in Kinloch so the Barbie had to settle for a dandelion or some kind of weed.

Ronnie was born premature and as a result had a slight cough from time to time. It didn't matter—he was precious and cute. He also kept himself well-groomed. He would not leave the house unless he was dressed for success. He ironed and creased his shorts. His shirts were starched. A popular outfit for him was a short-sleeve shirt, tucked into creased shorts, with a nice belt. He didn't wear the end of his belt hanging; he would fold it over or sew an extra loop on it to secure it. He was neat. He was clean. He dressed immaculately. When he was twelve, I remember him wearing a hot-pink suit. It looked custom made.

When I could convince Ronnie to hang in the yard, we would look for four-leaf clovers and dandelions to blow the white fluffy stuff around or turn them like helicopters. I was ready to jump from a tree into a pile of leaves. Ronnie was reluctant, but on the occasions when I could get him to cooperate, we'd sit up in that tree like Forrest Gump and Jenny, where once again nobody could find us. There were times I wanted to play touch football. Of course Ronnie was not interested in my tomboy ass. He used to ask me, "Why don't you wear skirts?" I told him, "I don't want nobody to see my booty if the wind blows it up."

My time with Ronnie made me think of Gladys Knight's version of "The Way We Were." *Everybody's talking about the good ol' days, the good ol' days…Come to think of it, as bad as we think they are, these will become the good ol' days for our children.*

Ronnie was my Pip and I was his Gladys. It was a wonderful childhood with him. Our early years together was our age of innocence.

We loved playing dress-up doll. He'd get a spoon for a microphone and books for Barbie's stage. We brought our own records. We'd put a 45 on. We'd have the doll singing Aretha's "Ain't No

Way." Every time Aretha would trill another riff in her voice, sending chills down my young back, we'd shake Barbie like she knew what she was doing. But white Barbie didn't know what a riff was. Then we started dancing, each of us with a Barbie in our hand. On that particular day, Ronnie's babysitter walked in. She snatched those dolls out of our hands so quick we didn't even realize what was happening. Before we knew it, we were in the car, on our way to church.

Once we got there, still full of energy, we went up to the choir stand and were acting a damn fool. Great Grandma Neil, disapproving, pointed her church fan at us, indicating that we should come sit down with her. There, we sat on the front pew with all those old ladies who didn't do nothing but look at Ronnie and I like *Umph, badass kids*. Because we were together, we didn't care what anybody said. We didn't care about nothing but being free and happy. And playing as hard as we could.

As we got older and were around town, we used to go to Miss Carter's shoe store. She lived in an old church that she had turned into a shoe store. All the shoes she carried had dropped off a truck, which made them affordable. Ronnie usually needed new shoes, because if something got on his shoes, rather than polish them, he'd work to buy a new pair. As I've said, he was a stickler about how he looked.

To earn money, Ronnie and I would babysit. One time we babysat Miss Ann's kids. She lived in this tiny apartment. The ceiling was so low that it was only inches away from our heads. There were roaches and leaking water and a whole bunch of shit that she couldn't afford to fix. It didn't bother us; we'd put those little fuckers to bed and lip-synched to our 45 records all night long.

As wonderful as our relationship was, I was number two in Ronnie's life. His mama was number one. He loved his mother, my aunt Gloria, and he'd talk about dressing her up like a Barbie doll. When he was in his teens, he dressed her up so well she made it into *Jet*. She was a print model. He kept Aunt Gloria looking like Lola Falana or Diahann Carroll from the TV show *Julia*. Aunt Gloria had style, beauty, and grace, thanks to Ronnie.

She was a real talker. And a fast talker. All of my aunties were fast talkers. I loved all nine of my mother's sisters: Catherine, Rosetta, Shirley, Margaret, Mary, Jean, Louise, Janice, and Gloria. They all spoke at the speed of light, never taking a breath:

OoooJennygirlyousocutelookatwhatyougoton.
Jennyalwaysrunninrountalkinboutshegonbeamoviestar.
Jennygetyourassupoutthatdirtandgetyourcrazyassinthishouse.
SomebodygoupinthatplumtreeandgetJennyouttatherefoshefall.
JennyJennyJennyJennysomebodygogetJenny.

All nine of my mama's sisters talked like that, and I loved it.

I tell young people today, if you ain't got no passion, you will die, become the living dead. Without passion, you're going to give up on yourself. Ronnie's passion was hair and fashion. Over time, Ronnie developed into a very talented hairdresser, which made him incredibly popular. He did almost everybody's hair in Kinloch. Ronnie wanted to be a star in his own right. He was as famous in Kinloch as I am in the world now. He was an everyman.

As amazing as Ronnie was, there were a few people who did not embrace him fully. Kinloch was a small town, and most of the folks were Christians. This made gayness unspoken. It was taboo. Folks who didn't approve of Ronnie's lifestyle would give him a dirty look and suck their teeth. They'd whisper "Punk-ass motha-Fucka." He gay as a three-dollar bill. He gay as a May breeze. It was a given that it was a great sin to be homosexual.

In the front row at church, we were in clear view of the pastor, the same one who molested me, and he would look at Ronnie with disapproval in his eyes. Ronnie would pay him no mind, and his discomfort would show only as Ronnie slightly rocking himself. He wasn't broken down by someone looking down on him. Ronnie handled himself. He was the light in those halls, not the darkness.

Sometimes Ronnie would get shade from the church ladies. In their big pink hats and kitten heels, they would brush by us, whispering under their stank breath about the way Ronnie liked boys. As if their shit didn't stink.

The number-one culprit was Miss Thompson. I couldn't stand her. She rolled up on my mama one time. *Bitch, you crazy.* My mama got sixteen sisters and brothers—you might not want to go nowhere near my mama. You messing with Ronnie because he's a kid. You don't want to get "jellybeaned," bitches (read *The Mother of Black Hollywood*).

WALKING IN MY JOY

Ol' snooty Miss Thompson was a heavy drinker. I would see her going in and out of the Threaded Needle, Kinloch's only night-club. She always had something to say about somebody while she was driving around drunk in that old raggedy-ass Deuce and a Quarter, swerving and curving all in the streets. I saw it with my own eyes. Ol' drunk-ass Miss Thompson.

The whispering from those fat-ass church women made my skin crawl. Right after they'd look down on Ronnie, they'd roll into the basement kitchen to stuff their faces with fried food, mac and cheese, and bread. Stuffing their shame down their throats carb after carb and dumping on boys like Ronnie. The way they laughed, cleared their plates, and raised their noses made me sick. In my opinion, deep down they hated themselves too much to save room for the joy Ronnie's spirit might bring them if they learned to accept him. They were afraid of his light. Even though they were sinning themselves, they pointed fingers at Ronnie and threw stones from their fat glass houses. It always seemed hypocritical, the way they put themselves on a pedestal, when the truth is they were hiding from their own shit.

Keep in mind fatty, *he who is without sin, let him cast the first stone, and I might bust yo head with a brick. Fuck a stone, bitch—I'll be throwing bricks.*

Every chance they got, the church ladies tried to put Ronnie down. They attempted to show him that he was ugly when he was not. They tried to instill hate inside his veins that just simply could not take hold. Ronnie was too sure of himself. Too spec-tacular. Too fabulous. Ronnie fought back with grace, by the way he carried himself. He wanted to be seen for who he was. More important, he wanted to be loved. And those of us who loved Ronnie protected him. And nearly everybody loved Ronnie. He didn't do nobody's hair who looked down on him. Bitches who did that couldn't get an appointment.

After I graduated from Webster, I was excited to leave the small-town mentality behind. I arrived in New York desperate to become a star in the 1980s. But leaving Ronnie, my biggest cheerleader, behind was difficult. I wanted to share all of this with him. As often as I could, I would buy a plane ticket for Ronnie to come visit me in New York. The first time he came was the first time he'd ever been on an airplane. He was eager to come because he knew I loved him more than anybody. He'd stay awhile each visit. He knew I needed him with me. I needed someone I was close to around me. I was on Broadway, and I knew Ronnie would help me to become who I wanted to be. He had supported my dream since we were children. Later in my career, he was the only person I could say this to and have it come across right: "Ronnie, I've made it." Some folks might have been envious or resentful, but Ronnie was proud of me. He knew all the hard work I had put in, honing my acting, dancing, and singing skills.

My apartment was at 55th and Broadway. Ronnie and I would get on bikes and ride from Columbus Circle to Harlem. To the Schomburg Center. To Sylvia's restaurant. We also took a lot of walks through Central Park. He learned to love Central Park like I did. We used the walks for healing whenever I didn't get a job or fucked up an audition. He'd pump me up. "Aunt Jenny, don't you worry about those stupid people. You're going to make it."

He always looked after me when he was in New York. Sometimes I'd go out drinking and carry on late and Ronnie would say, "Aunt Jenny, you know you got voice class tomorrow at nine. You may want to go to bed."

I recall saying that kind of thing to Liza Minnelli one time backstage in Los Angeles. She had given a concert and I could tell she was a little hoarse. I told her to get out of there, go home, and go to sleep. You got a show to do tomorrow night. Fuck these people. The great Liza Minnelli, Judy's baby, responded, "Jenifer, you're so right. You're so right." She looked at me like, *Wow, you care about that? You care about how I'm going to sound tomorrow night?*

Ronnie loved the smell of chestnuts roasting in the New York streets. Every time we passed a vendor, he'd always get a bag of chestnuts. I, on the other hand, loved the smell but couldn't eat them. I wouldn't eat anything off the street. I didn't care what kind of fire they were roasting on. Knowing I hated them, he teased me, "*Mmmm*, Jenny, this so good." "You look like a squirrel chomping down those nuts!" I'd reply. We'd laugh all the way down 7th Avenue.

His love of the chestnuts made me think of my first trip to New York. I was with my friend Susan Franks. After a long trip to Penn Station, a lamb kabob vendor was calling my name. As I reached for it, she said, "Are you insane, Jen?! That shit'll make you so sick. Let's go see the city." It was my first New York lesson.

On one visit, I took Ronnie to the World Trade Center, the Twin Towers. Once we reached the top, I would say things like, "I'm going to take this mothaFucka over. Just watch me." One hundred ten floors high in the sky, the view was like no other. I'd run Ronnie over to the side where you could see the East River and pointed. "That's the Brooklyn Bridge, Ronnie. P. T. Barnum, the circus guy, marched twenty-one elephants across that bridge. That's Jersey over there. I slept with a Jersey man. Over there's the George Washington Bridge. Yup, had him too."

Ronnie and I did cultural and fun things in New York. I would take Ronnie to gay club after gay club and we would sing at the piano. I was just a little-bitty famous then. I had done some club work around that time, and some people knew me and some didn't. I wanted to have fun walking and talking and singing. I didn't want anyone around me who couldn't sing. I liked harmonizing. When you sing with somebody, when you harmonize with somebody, you are instantly connected forever. You are making music, whether anybody else is hearing it or not. You are making beautiful music that goes somewhere out into the universe—and latches on to a nebulous development. If you couldn't sing, I didn't want you around me. Not in those days. (I got a lot of non-singers in my life now. I'm glad because I don't want them to join in anymore. At sixty-five, for those who don't know, I'm a solo fucking act. You ain't got to sing shit with me anymore. If you ain't Brandy

Norwood or Roz Ryan, you ain't got no business singing with me in these streets. Get the fuck on.)

Piano bar after piano bar, I'd get up and just show off. Ronnie would say, "Aunt Jenny, you act just like when we was kids. You just go in and take over places. But they loved you in there." I'd look at him and say, "Baby boy, there's not a gay man in the world who doesn't love your auntie. But none more than you." I'd kiss him on the cheek and off we'd go.

Ronnie was the beginning, and since then it has been me and a hundred million gay boys running around any town I set foot in. Whether I was home in Kinloch and Ronnie and I were dancing around the city or I was in New York performing on Broadway, it was gay boys who first dubbed me diva. It was gay boys who taught me my joy. I had never heard that word before. When I arrived in the Big Apple for the first time, I remember seeing two gay men holding hands and walking down the street in the Village. I was shocked and excited at the same time to see these boys love on each other so publicly at a time when it wasn't okay. Revolutionary. The gay men I surrounded myself with enriched my life, teaching me to *pas de bourrée* and *soutenu* and *grand battement* high-kick my ass across every stage that would have me. They literally taught me how to walk on air if need be.

When Ronnie visited, he wanted for nothing. The red carpet was rolled out. I allowed him to move around New York using my name. If I called a place to say my cousin was coming, the Red Sea was parted. That was when I was untreated for bipolar disorder and people knew that they would get killed if they didn't treat Ronnie right. I had a lot of power when I was unmedicated with a lot of repressed rage. Folks were scared of me.

Ronnie would go see Broadway shows, such as *The Best Little Whorehouse in Texas* and *Dreamgirls*, when I was on Broadway working on another show. I'd get him tickets so he wouldn't get bored. At the end of the night, we'd meet and talk about whatever show he went to see. A hair expert, he'd comment on the women's hairstyles. He'd describe the wigs in detail, knowing how much went into each look. He knew everything about hair and fashion. He talked about the hats they were wearing and the men's tuxedoes and how they were designed. He had that eye.

When he was in the city, he'd always do my hair. He would fluff it up and tease it as high as the Matterhorn. You couldn't say nothing to me. He made me glamorous. He wanted me to be as pretty as his Barbies. I wasn't going to be in all those gowns and dresses and stuff. I couldn't stand all that shit. *Bitch, I will not be uncomfortable so you can call me a lady.* Without him around, I would have to put on a hat and any sweat suit for an audition.

There was an excitement for life when we were together. An awakening. In those days, I NEEDED people around me. Somebody always had to be there. I could be alone, but if I went out into the world, somebody had to go with me. I wanted to talk about the floral displays in Macy's. I wanted to have fun. The early years in New York when you don't know anyone, except work relationships, are lonely. You want someone around who knows and loves you.

Ronnie and I would walk around New York City in our little outfits and window-shop just to laugh, naming every mannequin in the store, giving them backstories. "Look at the one in the bikini. Oh, she looks like Abigale from Kennedy Junior High School. She always thought she was cute. She kinda big now." We'd go on. "See that male mannequin? Oh, he one of these Ken doll looking mothaFuckas. Barbie can't be far. That tie he got on is cute, though. She look like Cher." He was a Cher fan. "Bet the bitch can't sing, though. She can't even open her mouth. Fake bitch."

In my twenties, on one of his first visits, I wanted to take him to the Russian Tea Room. Ronnie was reluctant to go into expensive restaurants. We'd read the menu outside the restaurant and I'd whisper, "Let's go in here with these rich white people!"

"Uh-uh, Aunt Jenny. This is expensive. We don't need to go in there. I'll cook something when we get home."

I'd insist, and he came to love the Russian Tea Room. I'd take him in there, and he would order the cheapest stuff. He was always humble in that way. He knew I had the money, but he never took it for granted.

The most beautiful thing about our time together as adults is that when Ronnie was in New York, he saw gay men being free. Later, when he traveled with me to concerts in San Francisco, he saw the same thing. This is when he truly started to grow up and come into his own. He took this energy back to Kinloch, growing into his free gay self.

The gay community helped me learn to love myself too. Their

glitter, glamour, and glow dominated every scene. Their artistry, spirit, and creativity were unmatched. They gave no fucks. They created space for me, a fun-loving loud diva in these streets.

Though the rest of society hadn't caught on yet, we knew that collectively Black women and the LGBTQ+ community had shaped the best parts of our culture. The parts filled with trust and hope and compassion and epic humanity.

The other side of the joy was the darkness of the AIDS pandemic that was running rampant through New York City in the '80s. I was losing friends left and right. When you are in your twenties and thirties, you don't expect to lose so many friends who are your age. If I learned what love was by sharing the sacred space with my gay friends, well then, you can be sure that I also learned loss. And if I was going through all of this, what must Ronnie be going through in Kinloch? AIDS was seen as a death sentence and gays were the carriers. Everyone was paranoid, just like we were in the early days of COVID.

No matter what was going on in the world, I would go home for Christmas. I didn't dare miss it. Ronnie wanted to show me off when I got home. He'd take me out to the clubs. I was famous in them parts. I was popular in St. Louis too. Being a local gal, the *Post-Dispatch* and the Black newspaper *The St. Louis American* would cover my shows. *Baggy Pants* had toured through St. Louis. *Eubie!* stopped in St. Louis. During these excursions, it was evident that Ronnie didn't want to be there and had outgrown Kinloch life. He wanted to be with me. "Aunt Jenny, when you going to take me with you?" At that point, he couldn't live with me in New York. I had moved to a studio apartment. And I was doing far too much fucking to have my gay cousin all up in there.

A few years later, my career was moving along at high speed, and I moved to California. One of my first invites was to Bette Midler's birthday party. I got so drunk. The reason I remember my age the year I moved out to LA is because I said, in a stupor, "Bheette, Imma be dirty-dree."

"You know what happened to Jesus when he was thirty-three, don't cha?" she responded.

Only Bette. Bitch. (Don't y'all tell her I said that.)

Ronnie would come out to California for short visits.

He was incredibly helpful when he was around. While working on *Strong Medicine*, I did plenty of AIDS benefits for the LGBT Community Center. My concerts raised money for kids who didn't have computers and assisted in getting therapy for the kids who'd been burned by their parents with cigarette butts because they were gay. We raised five hundred thousand dollars for a nonprofit Lily Tomlin was involved with that funded AIDS research. Ronnie was right by my side the entire time. We were front and center, publicly fighting the AIDS epidemic. That's right, it was about making this world a better place.

Every event I participated in when Ronnie was around, he did my hair and got a lot of exposure for it. He'd whip it over to the side like we had done with Miss Barbie back in the day. Those were the days I wore boas. Ronnie instructed me how to fling the boa so it wouldn't get caught in the ponytail. He was helpful in other ways too. He'd be the one out in the theater feeding me my lines or coming on stage to tell me if my lighting was good. He'd also give me straight-up practical advice: "Aunt Jenny, you might want to do the cartwheel the other way. You don't want to hit your foot on the piano. You don't want to scare the audience. Thinking you're going to hurt yourself."

In the fall of 1992, after scores of losses from AIDS, I went back to Kinloch to see Ronnie. When I saw him, he was still the same ol' Ronnie, and I didn't want him to live one second more without me. Even more than that, I didn't want to live without him. I invited him to come live with me in California. The invitation was more of a command—you know how I do.

I was living in a condo at this point. Ronnie lived there with me for six years. He worked for me and did hair on the side. Eventually, he moved out and into an apartment of his own in Hollywood. I wanted to make sure Ronnie was happy, so I flew his St. Louis boyfriend out to Los Angeles. I also shipped his car. It didn't last long, though. The boyfriend was too country, honey. *LA proved too much for the man*. He took a midnight train back to the muddy Mississippi River.

Then one day the earth shook. When Ronnie opened his apartment door to escape the Northridge earthquake and the pool's water smacked him in the face, I heard him curse for the first time. "A 7.2 earthquake! Aunt Jenny, the fat lady has sung." He went back to St. Louis.

My condo was condemned because of the damage from the earthquake. I stayed in FEMA housing, then moved back to my condo. They did a great job renovating it, but it wasn't enough to keep me there for long. I moved to Sherman Oaks and bought my first house. It was white and had a guesthouse in the back. I immediately thought Ronnie would love this. I had become legal guardian to my little sister, who was part of the Big Brothers Big Sisters program. Since Ronnie had raised his siblings, I thought he might want to help me with her. I imagined we'd have the best time together, just the three of us, young, determined, and free.

"I talked to God about those earthquakes. You get on back out here."

Ronnie hit the ground running. His salon, my guesthouse, was named Situations. He was serving lewks to the biggest names in Hollywood. He also serviced the white women in my neighborhood who worked their way into his chair. They'd be acting like they were watering the grass while being all nosy. "What do you do? Are you Jenifer's brother?" He did all kinds of hair—no matter the texture. He was doing a brilliant job and all of a sudden this mothaFucka nearly had a bigger career than I did. Ronnie showed me that all you need is a chair and a dream. He was thriving.

Having Ronnie around was like having a built-in best friend who lived right next door. We'd finish each other's sentences. He walked the red carpet with me. We hiked on mountain trails together. Ronnie was the physical manifestation of joy. He was so loyal. He still had Kinloch in him and would kick yo ass over Aunt Jenny.

Ronnie also had someone special in his life: Andy. Since Ronnie was the oldest child in his family and took good care of others, it was natural for him to cook and clean for Andy. They had been together for about a year and Ronnie was in love with him. I saw Ronnie one evening and he looked worn down as he told me about having Andy's mother over for dinner. Andy had not come out to his mother. Ronnie had tears in the corner of his eyes and a noticeable cough, and said, "Andy just did such a horrible thing, Aunt Jenny. He took my picture down so his mama wouldn't know who I was." To Ronnie, his photo being removed meant his boyfriend was ashamed of their relationship and ashamed of him. He didn't want to have to hide. This crime crushed him. Poor baby, he was so hurt he wanted to go back to St. Louis. I understood perfectly. I knew this particular pain well—betrayal, shame, and unbearable heartbreak.

Not too long after that, Ronnie invited me to breakfast at Jinky's. It was a farewell breakfast. A year before, his brother had hung himself, and Ronnie wanted to go home and be with his mother. I said how much I would miss him, swallowing down tears and hiding my sadness. Ronnie burst into tears. In that cry, he said, "I'm going to miss you." The "miss" could have been heard across the dining room. It was vomited in tears.

Six months later, I was in Florida campaigning for John Kerry when I got word that Ronnie was in a coma. I was shocked to learn he had AIDS. I'd had no idea he was HIV positive. Because of the shame our society baked into a positive HIV diagnosis, Ronnie never told anyone. Not even me. His girl. He kept his secret till the very end.

The man living in my guesthouse, my favorite cousin Ronnie, my whole heart, had been fighting HIV for years and never said a word. It pained me to know that my sweet cousin, while laughing with me every day, had been suffering in silence. He was giving me so much joy and simultaneously struggling emotionally and physically. The poor baby was frozen in denial. He never got treated.

I didn't quite know what to do and felt like I was in a trance for days. Ronnie was my friend, my brother—the son I never had. I missed him so much that I would call for him in the house, "Ronnieee." I yelled for him out of habit. It helped me feel him through the waves of my grief.

At Ronnie's funeral, I could barely hold myself together. I screamed like a hungry animal. It was piercing. I've never known pain like that in my entire life. I was completely broken open by the loss of Ronnie. When I got home from that funeral, I fell to my knees on the thick carpet in my closet and sobbed more than I had in my entire life. It was difficult to let go of the person I had shared childhood adventures with, the purity and joy we had experienced together. The loss of someone I trusted. The loss of someone to protect. The loss of someone who protected me. The loss of innocence.

I grieved Ronnie for a long time.

Everybody talks about the good ol' days . . .

DRAG QUEEN IN MY BASEMENT

I MOURNED MY PRECIOUS COUSIN Ronnie and moved forward, as we all must. As I learned to walk in my joy without Ronnie's physical presence, in every hummingbird, in every blossom, I felt his spirit. He was ever present. My career was moving so quickly, and before I knew it I was in New York City again; it was 2006, and I was performing in Shakespeare in the Park with Meryl Streep in *Mother Courage and Her Children*.

During my time in the city, on a late July night, I went to see a Broadway show called *Hot Feet* to support my friend Maurice Hines. After the show, I brought flowers backstage to his dressing room. We were laughing and hugging and just being, well, gay. Divas doing diva things. Performers doing performing things. Entertainers entertaining each other. Remembering how we used to spend our time in the back hallways of New York theaters with all of our ridiculously flamboyant friends. When I walked out the stage door, there was a little brown teenage-looking boy on his knees at my feet swearing he was my biggest fan. He heard I was at the show and followed me there, hoping for his chance at bumping into me. It was far too desperate, really, the way this boy fawned all over me, nearly in tears and praising me to the heavens.

Poor thing confessed to knowing every line and nuance of every movie and TV show I'd ever done, especially *Jackie's Back!*, which had premiered on the Lifetime channel in 1999. I ordered him off his knees. He bounced up from the ground so fast and continued singing my praises. Telling me I had inspired him, given him hope, shown him what it was like to be a rock-star diva.

"What's your name, little boy?" I asked as we left the theater together. He trailed behind me, keeping enough space to show me he wasn't crazy but staying just close enough to make me question his happy ass. "DJ Pierce," he responded.

DJ and I walked down the New York City sidewalks like we had known each other forever. This chiiiil' was quoting every line of *Jackie's Back!* Every line! He was so devoted. We got a slice of pizza, and I tossed him the script I was working on to shut him up. I could see in his eyes that he was over the moon about rehearsing Meryl Streep's lines with me. He did a flawless job. Not as flawless as I was doing reciting my lines back to him, but you already know that. After I learned my lines, I was done with this little boy. I stood up and said, "That's enough! Thank you, Baby." I hailed a taxi and he came in for the hug and I said, "Uh-uh, I ain't know you like that!" As a consolation prize I told him to come see me perform in *Mother Courage*. He was cute, but I got the hell out of there.

A few weeks later, as I walked out of my dressing room at the Delacorte Theater in Central Park, DJ was waiting for me again at the stage door. He had an old DVD in his hand of the film *Cinema Paradiso*. "I know this is your favorite film," he said to me, handing me the disk. Crazy mothaFucka. Reluctantly, I took it from his hand. As I looked into his eyes, I recognized myself. He wasn't a sycophant or a crazy stalker or even a desperate fan. He was just a sweet gay boy who was finding his way. He had been sent to me. Maybe by Ronnie. Maybe by God. Maybe it was all just one big fucking coincidence. But here he was.

"Well, come on, lil boy!" I said, ushering DJ through the stage door.

He scooted inside and talked his head off. He poured question after question on me: "What's it like to know Aretha Franklin? What's it like to perform on Broadway? With Meryl Streep? On set with the biggest stars in the business? And what about Double Entendre?!"

I stopped him in his tracks. I wiped off my makeup, looked at him, and said, "Uh-uh. What's your dream, baby?"

He became quiet for a moment. The last moment I'd ever hear silence from DJ. He wanted to move to LA, perform, be an actor.

"Okay, hush now," I said. "Well, I do need an assistant. What do you think?"

His eyes lit up like a Christmas tree.

DJ was from Paris, Texas. A little conservative town down south that had taught him he was a sinner. DJ didn't hide his pain, though. He lived it out loud. It's what I liked about him most. DJ was clear that a job like the one I was offering him would change his life in the exact way he wanted. He was open and honest about the things that had hurt him. It's the way he overcame them. He told me stories of his best friends being shipped away to conversion therapy centers in the middle of nowhere Texas. He showed me another ugly underbelly of being LGBTQ+ in America. He showed me the hate that still existed. See, I thought DJ might have had a different experience than Ronnie did. And to a certain extent, he did. To a certain extent, DJ's experience of being a gay boy was worlds away from Ronnie's. For starters, DJ had the freedom to be gay. He had the right to marry someone. He had the Oprah tapes and the self-help books and the LGBTQ+ Instagram influencers he could connect to at the push of a button. DJ had more than Ronnie had had, and still his day-to-day seemed to be full of prejudices. DJ experienced it differently—the AIDS epidemic was no longer the talk of the town, but there was still danger and, to this day, no cure. There were still whispers in churches and behind closed doors. People still called him a faggot and told him to mute himself down and conform. The difference was that DJ never did it. His light was just too bright. He was impossible to dim. An angel.

Like a Beverly Hillbilly, DJ packed up his 2003 Ford Explorer and drove through the tumbleweeds of El Paso before landing in Los Angeles to start his new job as my live-in assistant. During those first days when DJ lived with me in California, I learned about who he was. The sweetness inside his soul. How he cared for his family and friends and wanted to make the planet a better, more colorful place. I saw the potential of who he could be. This little gay boy with a big dream had a lot of learning to do. I felt the need to protect him. I wanted to trust him and take care of him and let him inspire me and be inspired. Family is the most important thing to DJ. I promised his mama and granny, who raised him, that I would treat him like my own. The po'bastid was stuck with me for the rest of his godforsaken life.

I moved DJ into my basement (otherwise known as the dungeon). He worked as my assistant while he pursued his dream of becoming a big star. "Deeeeeejayyyy," I'd shout in the morning. I'd get no response. Listen, y'all, that nigga can SLEEP. One morning I went down and DJ was hiding from a mouse the dog had dragged in, screaming at the top of his lungs. The next day he'd be listening to my old music collection, asking me every annoying question he could think of about it and taking notes on the ways I digested the world of entertainment. About two months into him becoming my assistant, he knocked at my door and told me he'd been accepted as a contestant on *RuPaul's Drag Race*. I'd had no idea he wanted to perform drag. Imagine my surprise. DJ, if you're reading this . . . NIGGA, weren't you supposed to be my assistant?!

DJ—yes, otherwise known as Shangela—was eager and excited by his talent. He couldn't wait to be better, but he didn't know exactly how. He was always learning, always growing, and, with my help, honing his craft. He reminded me of, well . . . me. I would familiarize him with the behind-the-scenes of Hollywood. The ins and outs of it. The mud beneath the glamorous river. DJ already had the talent. His energy is infectious. But yes, I did polish his country ass. Starting out, DJ performed at what seemed like every drag show in Los Angeles. He would be out all night, dressed to a tee, and get back to our place and sleep in his car from being so exhausted. Po'bastid couldn't even make it down the stairs to his bed.

One early morning, DJ was fast asleep in his beat-up truck. Let me pause here to say, this was the same car he drove cross-country. Let me pause again to say this is the same car he is *still* driving around LA and has named Ella. I hate this car. It's hideous. It leaks oil, and it makes no sense that he hasn't upgraded. Not to mention that this car shouldn't be parked in front of my Tuscan-style villa. Embarrassing-ass Ella.

Anyway, I had hired a team of white men to tend to my trees that year. That was a mistake. Why the HELL!!!!?????? did I hire a team of Republicans to tend to my garden!!!??? They turned on their machines and shouted disruptively. All this ruckus woke DJ up. Opening his eyes, DJ, dressed in full drag, sprinted out of his car and ran up my steps screaming and panicking. The lead landscaper, tall and potbellied with the clippers, looked like he had seen a ghost. As they came into the yard, none of them said a word to me, but each of them looked over their shoulder like someone was about to pull up on their asses. Po' bastids. Have you never seen a man with a beard dressed as a woman asleep in a truck parked on a street in Sherman Oaks? I sipped on my juice and made DJ do the same at the kitchen table, as was standard. His heels were higher than the journey to God, and his makeup was somehow still perfect, even after a night pressed up against the front seat of his shitty Ford. The red eye shadow winged out from his eyes to the heavens. It was art. Remind me to ask him who beat his face that night, y'all.

The glitter basically dripped from DJ as we enjoyed our green juice and pastries out on the lawn chairs. Every time one of the Republicans caught a glimpse of DJ, their eyes popped out of their head. Today was their lucky day in meeting a drag queen. They'd already met the head bitch in charge. I grabbed DJ. "You look FABULOUS, darling! FUCK 'EM!" I screamed. Then we blasted Chaka Khan's "I'm Every Woman" and danced the day away.

Later that day, I took Butters, my bichon frise puppy, out to puppy poop and caught a glimpse of DJ counting dollar bills in the basement. "ANNA MAE, WHAT YOU PLANNIN' ON DOIN' WITH ALL THAT MONEY, HONEY?!" I shouted, quoting a famous line from *What's Love Got to Do with It*. Usually DJ would shout back in perfect rhythm, finishing the scene. Instead he looked up, serious and not wanting to lose his count. "I'm saving up to buy my granny some carpet. Fifteen . . . sixteen . . .

seventeen . . . eighteen . . ." He continued counting and my heart completely melted.

I took DJ under my wing and we flew. Now he's hanging out with RuPaul and Gaga and Beyoncé. Just the other night I turned on the TV and saw his ass on the Jimmy Fallon show. A star. In fact, once we were in an elevator and he was recognized before I was. It took everything in me to not strangle him and the bitch who'd overlooked me. Nigga!!!! You know if you become a bigger star than me I'll come for your fucking ass. I'm kidding!! No, I'm not. Okay, let me stop. It overjoys me to see DJ be recognized. As he should be. DJ is a singular talent with a sensational soul.

DJ and I were finishing each other's sentences soon enough. It was customary for us to collapse on the sofa together and quote funny movie lines to bring us up out of our showbiz pity parties. We love and adore each other. The pain I felt from Ronnie's death would never go away, but DJ reminded me that my love wasn't wasted. My pain was merely the receipt, the proof that I had loved.

On top of that, DJ called me on my bullshit. He held me accountable. Our relationship was not just an act of me giving; it was a two-way street. DJ and his country ass was so real with me. He was never scared of me. Okay, once I had to push his ass in the pool for asking to be moved out of the dungeon. Seriously though, he saw my true heart.

The night of the Pulse nightclub shooting, DJ was performing drag at a bar in Los Angeles, California. He had gotten all dressed up and went off to dance the way he did mostly every weekend. Twenty-five hundred miles away at a gay bar in Orlando, an evil, hateful terrorist walked into the Pulse bar and killed forty-nine people, spraying bullets from his Glock 17. This was one of the deadliest mass shootings in US history. How many more of our LGBTQ+ community will be subjected to the same violence? How many other people can we justify being killed? I sat on the couch bawling my eyes out. Sick from it. Some of the people who stand for love most in this world had been taken down bullet by bullet. I thought of DJ performing some musical theater song on the other side of the city. I wondered if he was belting up there on that stage while another gay boy in Orlando with a big dream was being murdered in cold blood.

When DJ got home, we held each other. He told me that his friend Edward Sotomayor was one of those killed in the massacre. I was happy DJ was safe, but my heart bled for his friends.

When I think about the Pulse shooting, the only word to describe it is "hate." The killer was a man full of hate who walked into a bar full of love and tried to extinguish it. The entire LGBTQ+ community has been riddled with unimaginable pain at the hands of cowardly people. People so full of hate that they attempt to cut this indispensable group of people off at the root. I gravitate toward the LGBTQ+ community because even through that hardship, they have uncovered their freedom. That's right, those little gay boys and girls running around town unashamed are the epitome of the freedom we all seek in our everyday lives. Their over-the-top joy is unfamiliar because as a society we don't allow ourselves the same release. We don't allow ourselves to be divas. Our communities ostracize LGBTQ+ people because we are too scared to find out what might happen if we let them in. Fuck you and your homophobia. It's a new day; the gays have come to slay.

THE PULSE NIGHTCLUB SHOOTING VICTIMS

Edward Sotomayor Jr., 34

Stanley Almodovar III, 23

Amanda Alvear, 25

Oscar A. Aracena-Montero, 26

Rodolfo Ayala-Ayala, 33

Alejandro Barrios Martinez, 21

Martin Benitez Torres, 33

Antonio D. Brown, 29

Darryl R. Burt II, 29

Jonathan A. Camuy Vega, 24

Angel L. Candelario-Padro, 28

Simon A. Carrillo Fernandez, 31

Juan Chevez-Martinez, 25

Luis D. Conde, 39

Cory J. Connell, 21

Tevin E. Crosby, 25

Franky J. Dejesus Velazquez, 50

Deonka D. Drayton, 32

Leroy V. Fernandez, 25

Mercedez M. Flores, 26

Peter O. Gonzalez-Cruz, 22

Juan R. Guerrero, 22

Paul T. Henry, 41

Frank Hernandez, 27

Miguel A. Honorato, 30

Javier Jorge-Reyes, 40

Jason B. Josaphat, 19

Eddie J. Justice, 30

Anthony L. Laureano Disla, 25

Christopher A. Leinonen, 32

Brenda L. Marquez McCool, 49

Jean C. Mendez Perez, 35

Akyra Monet Murray, 18

Kimberly Morris, 37

Jean C. Nieves Rodriguez, 27

Luis O. Ocasio-Capo, 20

Geraldo A. Ortiz-Jimenez, 25

Eric I. Ortiz-Rivera, 36

Joel R. Paniagua, 32

Enrique L. Rios Jr., 25

Juan P. Rivera Velazquez, 37

Yilmary Rodriguez Solivan, 24

Christopher J. Sanfeliz, 24

Xavier E. Serrano Rosado, 35

Gilberto R. Silva Menendez, 25

Shane E. Tomlinson, 33

Luis S. Vielma, 22

Luis D. Wilson-Leon, 37

Jerald A. Wright, 31

/ WHAT PAGE ARE YOU ON? /

Ask the people down south about Katrina.

Ask the people in Puerto Rico about Maria.

Do some research on the Arctic and the Amazon,

Then ask yourself, What page am I on?

Ask the people in Europe about the heat last June,

The people in India about October's monsoon.

The polar bears, the whales, the koalas,

They're almost gone.

You need to ask yourself, What page am I on?

What page am I on?

CAPTAIN OF MY SHIP

I WAS ON THE *BLACK-ISH* SET the day and night of the 2016 election. Everyone was walking on eggshells, all day long, but I was certain we had nothing to worry about. *Surely this nation is not full of idiots. Surely we won't elect a pussy grabber.* As the hours went by, I could see the red states lighting up the map of the US on the set's television.

When we wrapped, I drove home with a certainty in my heart that by the time I woke up in the morning they would all have turned blue. When I opened my eyes the next day, I knew I had misjudged the situation from the quiet of my neighborhood. There was a chilling hush in the air. This was Sherman Oaks, for God's sake—a blue neighborhood inside a blue city inside a blue state. If we had won, I would have heard about it by now. I was numb. We had lost.

As I lay in bed, I heard a scratching at my door. It was DJ. I waved him over and he crawled under my covers, holding me, shaking with fear. It felt like the United States of America had now been occupied by a new Nazi regime.

Every horrible thing that humanity had experienced came back to life the moment Donald Trump was elected. His presidency became a black hole of evil. First it was the Muslim ban, halting Syrian refugees and barring citizens from seven other Middle Eastern countries from entering the United States. Next it was his random and concerning covfefe tweets. He was egging on the Proud Boys, offering to pay bail for anyone who sucker punched Black Lives Matter protestors outside his rallies. He was claiming there were some "very fine people on both sides" in Charlottesville following violent attacks from neo-Nazis on the alt-right.

It was around this time when I felt the need to get away from it all and went on a cruise ship to Antarctica. I was full of world-changing ideas but wanted to sit with myself a bit before fully diving in. I desired to take some time to see the grandeur of sights rarely seen. I needed to get a fresh look at the world—or lure a handsome, single young man to my cabin. At sixty-two, I was not quite still a brick house but only a few inches off. All right, a *whole lot* of inches off, but fuck y'all.

On the ship, there was a group of young performers from all over the world—Germany, Turkey, South Africa, Argentina, Puerto Rico, Japan. They followed me on Instagram and were familiar with my political savvy. They were a gaggle of twentysomethings, fawning over me and treating me like a queen. Just what Mama needs—a captive audience while traveling solo. Surprisingly, they were engaged in the politics of the world too. From cruising damn near seven continents, these kids had witnessed so much. Several of them told me stories about the adventures, cultures, and perspectives they had gathered. Each night our conversations surrounding climate change came up more and more. We talked about how New York City was sinking. The place I used to tap dance, sashay, and terrorize subway stations with my booming voice would one day be underwater. And God help Florida, New Orleans, and the other fifty states too. We also talked about Greta Thunberg, the prolific teen climate activist who led the School Strike for Climate campaign.

They told me how they perceived the US since the election of the Orange Man. One of them, from Chile, went on about how disgusted she was by the American people. She had seen the protests and the police brutality, and the white men and women screaming "Build a wall!" at the border. She informed me that she used to dream of living a life in the US. Now she was happy to just stay put. She was disturbed by our nation's inability to unite and get our shit together. These kids reminded me of our collective and individual power to create change. These kids made sure I remembered. Hmmmm, I'm listening!

Oh, how we had fallen. I was disturbed by our nation's crumbling reputation under the Orange Man.

They also shared the way they themselves were stepping up to the plate for change and social justice through fundraising, protesting, and having hard conversations with the people closest to them.

One night I couldn't sleep and found myself staring at the stars on the top deck. I was contemplating our existence and our power to either make or break the planet. As I turned, heading back to my cabin, I noticed the captain sitting alone, enjoying a late-night nosh.

I approached him timidly. Well, as timidly as I approach anything. Two captains standing face-to-face.

He was French and sexy. Help me, Black Jesus! It was mighty dark up there, and I thought for a moment, *Why not?!* Then I saw the ring on his finger and shut the shit down. His face lit up, and he admitted he'd heard from some of his staff that I was a celebrity. After my humble "*Oh, chile, please*" confirmation, his face scrunched. In the thickest French accent he pointedly said, "Miss Lewis, my crew tells me you're a famous actress in the United States, but I also hear you're an activist. Is that true?"

There was something about the way he'd said the word "activist," that struck an entire symphony playing in my soul. The way he'd said it made it seem as though it was my destiny. I sat there for a moment, digesting the word. Swallowing every bit of it and deciding on how to truly wear the label.

Then I responded kindly to the captain and nodded my head. "Yes, sir, I am." After all, I have worn an Afro most of my life. And if an Afro doesn't say "activist," then what does?!

"Then let me please ask you to go back to your country and tell whoever will listen that we are in fact in trouble. The Arctic is melting at the speed of light."

"You can count on me, Captain. You ain't said nothin' but a word, baby. Now you might want to get your fine ass back to the front of the ship before this bitch hits an iceberg."

He walked away and I was left there, staring up at a tiny crescent moon smiling at me. I smiled back it. I dashed to an empty lounge with a piano, and without even turning on a light. I wrote the song "Climate Change Is Real." The next day I would boldly post it on my Instagram feed:

Climate change is real.
Destroying the planet wasn't part of the deal.
Climate change is real.
Destroying the planet wasn't part of the deal.
The kids are gonna need clean air.
We can't sit on our asses like we just don't care.
The whales are throwing themselves ashore,
Showing us they can't take it anymore.
The fire, the wind, the flood—
Haven't we seen enough blood?
Climate change is real.
Destroying the planet wasn't part of the deal.

I sat there at the piano resolved, feeling like a revolutionary. I had a platform and a plan.

A few weeks later, I found myself at Tyler Perry's studio opening. What an accomplishment this was. He built his studio in one of the poorest Black neighborhoods in Atlanta. He wanted the young people there to see that they had it in them to achieve at the highest level. It was intentional that the land the studio stood on was once a Confederate army base, which means that at one point in time there were Confederate soldiers plotting how to keep millions of Black people enslaved. Now a Black man owned that land. Ain't karma a bitch?!

Tyler was making a huge statement. For years the entertainment industry has profited off our Black and brown artists, who have rarely seen the economic benefits of their success. Now Tyler Perry would be the first Black man to own his own studio. For so long Black artists were sent the message that we don't deserve a seat at the table. By opening his own studio, Tyler Perry was building his own table, one that economically empowered everyone.

Tyler's was the party of the century. Everybody was there, dressed to the nines. Instead of using that time to schmooze, carry on, and dance the night away, I stalked every A-list celebrity and politician and asked them to make a video urging people to vote. "Get your ass out and vote!" was my battle cry. By the time I left, I had a collection of videos on my phone that screamed "VOTE!" by Hollywood's most wanted: Samuel L. Jackson, Oprah, Bill Clinton, Beyoncé, Stacey Abrams, Taraji P. Henson, Viola Davis, Joy Reid—the list goes on and on and on. I wanted to use my platform for a cause.

Back in LA, after Tyler's event, I continued my activism. I sang with Brandy at the Women's March, the largest single-day protest in US history, insisting that fifty million of us would march down to the border and tear down that wall if the Orange Man dared to build it.

On the drive home, I pulled over to get gas on Ventura Boulevard. I overheard two young girls talking about a brewing feud between Nicki Minaj and Cardi B. They leaned in, challenging each other and screaming "TEAM NICKI!" "NO, TEAM CARDI!!!" I laughed. I couldn't believe this small fight between these two women had sparked a national conversation, given all the important issues that were going on in the world. It was everywhere, two Black women tearing each other down. I don't believe in publicly displaying grievances. Are either of these women doing anything for the cause? I'm asking, Is this how you want to use your celebrity?

At home, I dipped into my pool and swam laps obsessively. *What can I do?* I had a platform and I wanted to use it for good. Then it came to me: the Emmys were in just a few weeks, and I could start a conversation about social justice with my wardrobe. I got out of the pool, then made a video pleading with Cardi B and Nicki Minaj to stop the hate and start helping me activate the millennials to care about causes that affected them. When I was done, I drove right over to The Grove in West Hollywood to find my Emmys outfit. On the way over, I saw a big Nike billboard with Colin Kaepernick's face on it. That year I decided to ditch the fancy gown and dressed head to toe in Nike to support Colin Kaepernick and his mission against racial injustice and police brutality. When I showed DJ what I had bought, his eyes nearly rolled out of his head. "Uh-uh, honey, you need to blingify that thing." Within minutes there were five drag queens at my door, ready to bedazzle. I walked the carpet with my head held high, remembering: Trayvon Martin, a young man who was brutally murdered by George Zimmerman in Florida in 2012 over a bag of Skittles; Michael Brown, a Ferguson teen who was fatally shot in 2015 by officer Darren Wilson; Sandra Bland, who was suspiciously found dead in her jail cell in Texas after she was unnecessarily stopped on the side of the road and arrested. We all saw the video. We all know they killed her. Sadly, the list goes on.

With every evil tweet Trump sent, I followed up by warning America that if we didn't vote, democracy as we know it would surely end. I was becoming comfortable with my passion for change. I could feel my power growing with each act. I could see tangible change on the horizon. Nobody was going to be grabbing us by the pussy anymore.

DON'T LISTEN
TO
THE TROLLS

Don't listen to the trolls.

Get out to the polls.

Join the debate

In these United States.

You gotta be in it

If you want a new Senate.

Here's the quote:

Get your ass out and vote.

Get your ass out and vote.

Hey, get your ass out and vote.

If you want to see change,

Get your ass out and vote.

These are not dark times,

These are awakening times.

So get your ass out and vote.

TWO-OH TWO-OH, WAIT A MINUTE, THO

IT WAS DECEMBER 31, 2019. Begrudgingly, I went to see the latest *Star Wars* movie with my old college posse. They were all fans. I was not.

"Come on Jenifer," they pleaded. "Stop being a diva and come see *Star Wars* with us." So I went but, made them promise we would return home early before all the assholes got drunk and started driving.

My New Year's Eve tradition is to read and review my entire journal from January to December. What did you do with a whole year, Jenny? Where d'ya go? Why'd you go? Who'd ya help? Who'd ya cuss out? And above all, Who'd ya sleep with? Okay, Who didn't ya? Just kidding, y'all. No I'm not.

I relived the heat in Hot-lanta while filming *Christmas on the Square* with my beloved Dolly Parton. I read on about the high-lights of campaigning for Kamala Harris, and how sad I'd gotten when they announced John Lewis had pancreatic cancer. I remi-nisced about the twentieth anniversary of the movie *Jackie's Back!* I was reading about some senators and UFOs and the awful Or-ange Man. My eyes started to get real heavy. I drifted off and . . .

. . . found myself in a black forest. A place that has stardust on tree branches and a night so black I could barely see. I walked through the black forest self-assured, as if I knew where I was going and as if it belonged to just me. For some reason, I began skipping. That's right, there I was, Jenny Lewis, skipping through a black magical forest. Up and down and up and down through the black forest. Thank God for my two breast reductions.

Suddenly I saw a glowing green light illuminating the trees ahead in the distance. Now look, I'm as curious as the next fool, so I skipped my happy ass a little faster toward it. I never have been able to step away from the spotlight, have I?

Anyway, as I made my way toward the green light, I spotted a small silver saucer-like object hovering a few inches above the ground from where the light was coming. Biiiiiiitch, I found the extraterrestrials?!?!?!? I always knew I'd find 'em. I approached timidly—well, as timidly as I ever approach anything—and was met by a tiny little green fucker with an enormous head. He had tiny little green arms, tiny little skinny legs, and stubs for fingers and toes.

I said, "Good Lord, baby, how you doin'?!"

He said, in his robotic baby-alien voice, "You are the diva, we presume."

"Well, baby," I shot back, "I'm sure I'm the only diva in these black forest streets today. What exactly do you need?"

He went on to spin some story about how I had been abducted by evil forces from his home planet, Divaretus, and that, well, I was their queen. Truly it was no surprise that I was the queen of an unearthly planet. I mean, really, my whole life had been a precursor to this moment. It explains my behavior all these years. I should have known.

"We have searched the galaxies for you, Queen Lewis," the little alien creature said. "Upon your birth, you were beamed by evil forces to planet Earth. Please return to planet Divaretus and assume your rightful place upon the throne. The Divaretian people need you to come home."

I cackled. HA! *Return to planet Divaretus? Does William Morris have an office up there? Does ICM rep any talent on planet Divaretus? CAA? What's that? No? Okay, well then, little sir, my ass will be staying right here on planet Earth.*

"Now, listen. Mama can't do that, baby," I said to this tiny little green alien.

He then proceeded to kneel before me on one little tiny knee. I said, "Oh I see, so you gon' go Kaepernick on a bitch. Don't y'all be fuckin with him cause we need his ass here on earth."

"Queen Divaretus, we are here to protect you. The year two-oh two-oh is upon us. There will be great pain this year. There will be a great sickness, a great war, a burning. That which you call 'the white people' will rise up. Beware the beast," he warned.

Now, I know this tiny little green fucker did NOT just say the white people are gonna rise up. I cackled. "HA!!!! White people would never do that. They don't protest! They have everything!!! What the flying saucer fuck are you talking about, Mr. Greenie?! I don't wanna hear about no pandemic. Carry your miniature ass back to outer space before I slap you upside your abnormal big-ass head! All this apocalyptic shit. I'm Jenifer Lewis. I ain't dying for nobody, Nigga!!!!"

I rolled my eyes and flat-out refused to believe any of this green bullshit. I am not about to be told what to do by this tiny little ET-looking ass!

"Queen Divaretus, I have heard the legend of the difficult diva that you are, originating from Divaretus, but I never thought it could be true. Hold, please, for my commander. She will take it from here."

"Awww shit! Okay, Greenie! Go get ya gurl! I ain't scared!"

He squinted his eyes and shook his big bobblehead in utter irritation at me. Before he boarded his silver saucer back to planet Divaretus, he turned around, looked at me, gave me the middle finger, and said, "Good luck, Queen Bitch!"

Hmph, I thought. *My nigga. We really are from the same planet.* I turned on my heels.

Just when I was sure the alien invasion was over, the ship

began to turn all types of colors. A rainbow of reds, greens, and blues from the godliest palette. Fog filled the air. It smelled like a sweet plate of beignets and a little bit of peach cobbler baking in Kinloch, all mixed together. Familiar and yet absurd. I stopped in my tracks and heard a booming voice call to me.

"Stop walking away on those that you call 'feet,'" the voice called out in surround sound.

Those that I call feet? What the fu—? I turned again. Lo and behold, there she was. Greenie's commander. The bitch looked just like me too. Short, 'fro out, shoulders back, titties first. She even had a small scar that mirrored the one I had over my left eye. But she was green, with beautiful scales all over high cheekbones and a face that glittered in the light through the thick fog. She wore a tight leather jumpsuit and a pair of fuzzy red slippers. Y'all picturing this shit?

"Well, who the fuck are you?!" I shot to her, puffing out my chest, making sure I established the pecking order in these space-ship streets.

"I am commander of planet Divaretus, Shaniqua Ben Kanobi." Then in perfect Ebonics, she said, "Queen Lewis, you 'gon hafta calm yo royal ass down and listen 'cause we got some shit to say and then we gotta go 'cause we runnin' outta gas. Gas prices on Divaretus ain't no joke. They done gon up to 200 dollah a gallon." Did this bitch just break character!?!?! Back in her alien voice, she continued. "I bow down to you, my queen, and all you do on this planet Earth that you love so much."

WALKING IN MY JOY

"AW YEAH!!! BOW DOWN, BITCHES!!!" I said.

"Now, my underling tells me you wish to stay."

I nodded my head and folded my arms. "I'm a STAR here on Earth, Commander! I'm staying, I'm staying, and you and you and you, you're gonna love me!!!!" Yes, I broke into *Dreamgirls*. What else could I do?!

Her eyes were closed while she whispered to herself. Then she opened her eyes. "I have a message for you. The Divaretus tribunal has proclaimed you should indeed remain here on this blue gem called Earth. You are, in fact, needed [as if I ain't just said that]. Your Royal Highness, you must answer the call. The next few years will be trying. You are The One. You are the warrior of this planet. You *must* fulfill your duty and save the planet. You *must* fulfill your duty and save the world, save the people, save the children. Protect yourself. Protect your heart. Earthlings did not come into the dimension filled with love. They came into the dimension to learn why they hate themselves. This hate has been unleashed, but you, Queen Divaretus, can heal these people. We now encourage you to stay if you continue your mission. Do you confirm?"

I nodded my head yes, confirming. Now, I ain't saying this green diva had me moved to tears, but I'm not NOT saying that neither.

She bowed and whispered, "Okay then, Queen Lewis, we will leave you here on Earth. There will be so much pain, but humankind will overcome."

She lifted a giant handbook out of her front pocket. I don't know where that damn thing was hiding since her leather jump-suit was skintight. Slut. She handed it to me. I opened it and read the first few pages. It was full of phrases that held the most wisdom I have ever read.

Love yourself so that love will not be a stranger when it comes.

Everything that occurs, occurs for the purpose of enlightenment.

When the teacher can bow to the student, the real work can begin.

Human laughter creates the vibrant colors of nebulas.

Walk in your joy.

Tell Keisha she still owes you five dollars.

And that's when my eyes opened. It was January 1, 2020. Queen Divaretus and all her glory had been but a dream. I wrote down everything I could remember, wiped my eyes, shook off the alien invasion, and pulled myself out of bed. Before my feet hit the ground, I cackled again. YASSSSSSS! Queen Divaretus in these streets.

My toes touched the floor and so it began. The year two oh two oh.

THAT'S ENOUGH

Everybody check your soul at the Super Bowl.

That's enough!

Take away their fun

Before they shoot your son.

That's enough!

Our ancestors kneeled in the cotton fields.

That's enough!

Whites, Blacks, Jews, we've gotta refuse.

That's enough!

Get a backbone

Before a bullet comes down on the back of your own.

That's enough!

Before another hate crime,

Be the gladiators of our time.

You are the gladiators of our time!

You want a standing ovation?

Take a knee for the next generation.

FUCK THE FALLING YEARS

LIKE A GOTDAMN FOOL, a few weeks before I left for *The Mother of Black Hollywood*'s book tour, I invited my dear friend Vanessa to my house to stay with me. I should've known better because Vanessa just so happens to be a worrier. I'm telling you, this bitch worries about *everything*—from paying the bills on time to lightning striking her ass, while shopping indoors at the mall, on the basement floor. She was the one bipolar bitch I held on to after my own treatment. That kind of friendship is just so hard to get rid of. She also gossips a lot—she wants to know the ins and outs of who's fucking who in Hollywood, which one of our college roommates "didn't make it," and how much money is in the bank accounts of every person who comes through the door of my home. When she isn't running her mouth, she's complaining about every ounce of fat on her body, while sitting there eating a Hostess cupcake. Having this energy around, especially in your home, is never the right thing. As the saying goes, "After three nights, houseguests start to smell like fish." Well, let's just say this bitch started stinking the moment she unpacked her shit. But I still love her anyway.

A few days into her stay, my backyard became infested with ants. Go figure, her worrisome energy manifested these little creepy-crawlers. In a rush to remove the fuckers, prompted by Vanessa's overly dramatic loud-ass screaming (I should talk), I flew directly onto the concrete, falling and landing hard on both of my knees. Now look, y'all, I'm not blaming her, but trust me when I tell you, if ugly energy is around you, ugly energy is gonna get on ya. Hell, not only on ya but inside ya.

I immediately rushed to my orthopedic's office, where Dr. Yun told me that I had officially entered my "falling years." Falling years? Let me say that one more time: falling years. Fuck the falling years. I was warned that I would have to pay more attention to my steps than I usually did, that I would have to take extra care, that it was time to be meticulous with where and how I spent my energy. Let's just say I sent Vanessa off to skedaddle. I couldn't have no more of that negative shit getting on me. Neither my spirit nor my knees could handle any more.

As I iced my knees and swore off the falling years, I received an email from my manager with the schedule for my book tour. It looked something like this:

THE MOTHER OF BLACK HOLLYWOOD
BOOK TOUR SCHEDULE

New York

Philadelphia

Washington, DC

Los Angeles

San Diego

San Francisco

Baltimore

Miami

Fort Lauderdale

West Palm Beach

Chicago

Detroit

Flint

New York

Los Angeles

St. Louis

Atlanta

Denver

Los Angeles

OMG?! Oh hell naw. If I had really looked at my book tour schedule before it was solidified, I would've told my team hell to the naw, but I guess I loved them too much. And I trusted them too. This was my first book and it took me three years to write it.

Amistad, an imprint at HarperCollins, offered me a lovely deal to publish it to boot. Writing a book was the hardest thing I had *ever* done. In *The Mother of Black Hollywood*, I had literally vomited the horrors I'd held inside my entire life. But then again, when have you ever vomited and not felt better?

My biggest prayer was "God, help me to help somebody help themselves." If I was going to be crawling from city to city, then I needed to be in my tippiest-toppist shape.

I hadn't been on the road in years. Come hell or high water, I was not going to limp onto any stage with my arthritic knees looking like Quasimodo or Dracula's fucking assistant Igor. The last time I had traveled extensively, my knees were so much more youthful. Now if I sat down, I hardly wanted to get back up. Age is a motha, ain't it?

Aging is the process of becoming older.
Yes, my hair is starting to thin.
Don't do that, baby.
The Afro is back in.
Let's talk about the eyes,
The crow's-feet.
Ouch, there's a stye.
They call it adult acne.
Please, Black Jesus, tell me why.
Now, what the fuck is going on here with my neck?
I look like a Chinese shar-pei,

Titties racing to my knees.

Oh, and by the way,

That tire around my waistline inflates tighter day by day.

This is bullshit, y'all

Can't even see my vajayjay.

Last time I had sex and moved to change positions,

I pleaded, "Hold on. Hold on. Baby, let's take an intermission."

The feet, the feet, the plantar fasciitis,

The joint of my right big toe, riddled with arthritis.

So there you have it.

I'm aging from head to toe.

What's a little hair thinning?

I can just go buy a 'fro.

As for sex, together we can make it work.

Errrbody in the world knows I can still twerk.

Trust me, y'all, aging ain't so bad.

Just remember your life is your song,

So you take good care

Who knows you might just live long.

I immediately booked a stay at the Optimum Health Institute, to cleanse my soul, detox my gut, and strengthen my muscles. If I was going on a tour like this, well then, gurrrl, I was gonna be on my A game. Y'all know Auntie don't play-play.

Hellishly healthy. That's how I would describe the Optimum Health Institute in Lemon Grove, California. Each time I go, in an attempt to lose ten pounds and feel ten years younger, people are buzzing about being half dead from the intensity of the mandatory body cleanse or insanely happy from having just completed the war that is the Optimum Health program. All the walls are a beige color, pushing the notion of serenity on you. It gets me looking and feeling all the way right in these streets. It is both a blessing and a curse that I've discovered this rustic little health haven.

My cleanse was to be seven days of nothing but raw foods and green juice entering every hole I could name in my body. And I mean *every* hole. Picture *Nine Perfect Strangers*, a show about a wellness retreat gone wrong, with a lot less blood and a lot more wheatgrass. I was sure that by the end of the week, I'd be prepared to hit the road for my book tour.

The day I arrived on the Optimum campus was easy. I was presented with my regimen of an all-raw, tiny-portioned diet. I was determined to start the program like an Olympian. No carbs! No problem! The next day was tougher, but still, I was unstoppable. It was day three that got me into trouble. You see, on day three I woke up HUNGRY. Ravenous like a hyena in the Serengeti. I thought of my loose muscles and the little bulge/pooch in my stomach and that was enough to keep me from cheating on the program (yes, fuck y'all, I care about my waistline). By four o'clock I was living on a prayer. Exhausted. Desperate for the In-N-Out burger I allow myself once a year. By four thirty I was barely breathing, dragging my ass over to the wellness center for my first wheatgrass enema of the stay.

Yes, you heard me correctly. The Optimum Health clinic strongly suggests at least TWO (2) wheatgrass enemas daily. The Institute swears by this shit. The Triticum aestivum plant—wheatgrass—is a superfood. As a microgreen or in juice form, it's highly regarded in the wellness community as a potent health food with amazing benefits, promising to boost digestion, metabolism, and immune system responses.

I walked into the center boldly, where a nice blond lady named Karen escorted me into a private room. Not that type of Karen who refuses to wear a face mask for her five-minute trip to the supermarket during a pandemic, though. This Karen was lovely. Overly nice. The walls in this particular room were painted eggshell white. The neutrality of it all was meant to make visitors feel safe. Surprisingly, it was working. Blondie Karen laid a human-size towel on the table and instructed me to get undressed, lie on my left side, and relax. I followed her directions. Well, minus the relaxing part. You try relaxing while some white lady pumps some green juice into your anus. She asked me to clench my butt cheeks for five minutes while the wheatgrass did what it was meant to do.

She looked at me, impressed, after we were done. I gave her a wink, thinking bitch, please. Mama knows what she's doing, with her buttcheeks. I gathered myself, got dressed, and shuffled out just as quickly as I had come in. As I walked out to the parking lot, I heard a loud set of footsteps behind me.

"Miss Lewis, wait!" she shouted. "I meant to remind you: no food and no drink for the rest of the day, and be prepared for bowel movements in about two hours."

My life was over. NO food. NO drink. My stomach began to eat itself. I sat in my room terrified for the next hour and a half, anticipating the forewarned shits. I waited and waited and waited. Then, concluding that my body was too godly to be betrayed by the wheatgrass, I snuck off campus and took myself to a movie at a strip mall nearby. It was just ten minutes away. I ordered myself a mini-size butterless, saltless popcorn bowl. This was basically not food at all, I had convinced myself.

As I sat down, I giggled defiantly. *I ain't no bitch, Blondie*, I thought as I shoved a handful of popcorn into my mouth. *I ain't no bitch.* Shortly after the movie started, I felt a rumble and a tumble in my tummy. I dropped all the kernels to the floor and escaped the theater. I, being a celebrity and all, have reached the point in my life where I refuse to shit in public restrooms. It is one of the few bougie qualities I've picked up. I reached my car, convinced that I could perform my clenched butthole trick again for the next ten minutes to get back to the campus. As I pushed the ignition, I came to terms with how wrong I truly was. The ignition did not ignite. I did. I discovered a new meaning for "pedal to the metal."

When I was a child, my aunt Membry always told me to keep a pot in the back seat of the car in case of an emergency. She used to drive us back and forth to daycare and never wanted to stop for a bathroom break, so when we needed to go, she'd pull out the pot from her trunk and we'd do our business. When we were done, she'd toss it out the window carelessly, splashing whoever was on the side of the road, and kept it moving. The bitch was brilliant. I pulled out my emergency pot. Unbuttoned my pants. And crawled into the back seat.

Just then a frazzled white mother pulled into the spot next to mine. She parked her car, swung her door open, and ran out of the vehicle. Her six-year-old redheaded son was left in the back seat, staring directly at me. The inside of the car was steaming hot. Prior to that moment I used to think my shit didn't stink, but well . . . Windows fogged from my sweat and the breath of my screams. I was smacking the window, pleading with God for dear life. It seemed the kid thought I was waving at him. He waved back, watching with joy while I moaned violently and shat my brains out all over the back seat. I'm so sorry, little Timmy. Po' lil bastid had to witness me in one of my most vulnerable moments.

THE MOTHER OF BLACK HOLLYWOOD

AFTER MY STAY AT THE HEALTH INSTITUTE, I was ten pounds lighter and ready to take on a twenty-five-city tour. First stop, NYC, Here I come!

I packed talent, confidence, courage compassion, vulnerability, and a large container of humility and set out on tour. *Black-ish* had adjusted my schedule, given me their blessing and a big old "Get on outta here and make us proud." It was time to step out of my comfort zone. I was going to meet the people face-to-face. The book had received rave reviews from everybody, everywhere. Oops, I did read that four people didn't like it. I'd like to respond to those comments right now. Fuck all four of y'all.

My song "For the Book" (sing it with me!!) had already gone viral.

These fools told me to rap for my book,
So I tap, tap, tap for my book.
Red lips for my book,
Titties and hips for my book.
I hit a high note for my book.
Now you're woke for my book.
Rum-pa-pum-pum for my book!
You bitches better run for my book.
I got a plate and a pig,
'Cause my book gon' be big,
My book gon' be big.

Landing in the Big Apple felt more natural than I ever could have imagined. It was like I had never left. One whiff of the nasty November garbage air and I was home. As you can tell by now, I carry home with me everywhere I go. But New York is different for me. This was the place that had polished me up and taught me to be the Jenny Lewis that was destined to accept her undeniable stardom. Plus, one can never forget sex at the top of the Empire State Building. After all these years, there are just some things that will never be undone. When I got to Manhattan it was like I was a subway rat returning to my pack, as smooth as can be.

I can't say it enough: just eleven days, bitches, after college graduation, Hurricane Lewis hit these Broadway streets. This is the reason New York will always be home for me.

When I got my first Broadway gig, I called home to tell my mama the news. She said she always knew I'd be a big star and hung up the phone. She didn't even give me the chance to tell her how much that meant to me. Years later, my sister Robin told me that, after the call, Mama told them I'd be home before I could blink twice. "I'm gonna let little Jenny do that acting thing," she said, "but if she ain't gonna be the big ol' star she says she gonna be, she can just come on back home and be a substitute teacher over at McCluer North High School over in Florissant."

Oh, Mama, always the optimist.

I was standing on the curb at JFK, imagining the first big book event; reciting a few stories, doing a song and dance, and then moonwalk the fuck off that stage.

New York City was hustling and bustling, just like I remembered. The air was stiff. The rats were ratting. There were tall model-esque bitches running the streets. It was all so fabulous.

The first venue on the tour was the Triad Theater on 72nd Street. Formerly known as Palsson's Supper Club, Steve Mc-Graw's, and Stage 72. The Triad Theater is an iconic cabaret-style performing arts venue. If I am anything, I am born from cabaret. I basically learned how to say "That's showbiz, baby" in the back halls of that theater.

The Triad was everything I could have dreamt of for my first performance. It gave me that old NYC feeling I fell in love with all those years ago.

As we got closer to the theater, I spotted a line extending two blocks around the corner. All these people queued up like sardines, and it was cold outside.

"Po'bastids," I said to my driver. "What could they possibly be waiting for this time?!? The new iPhone?"

"You, Miss Lewis," he said. "They're waiting for you." Looking at me in the rearview mirror, he smiled.

Waiting for me? It couldn't be. I had seen lines like this outside the Delacorte Theater, wrapping around Central Park back in the early '80s, but that was when I was performing a big show with big names at a big theater. On *black-ish* I was their grandma. Here, today, I would be myself. And they still had shown up for *me, me, me, me, me, me, me, me*. They liked me. They really liked me. Po' Sally. I was an author. Jeeeeeeeesus. An author. *Go on, Jenny*, I thought, as we pulled up to the stage door. I got out of the car, waved at those precious people in line—politicians, social workers, doctors, lawyers, students, all dressed up to see and hear from little ol' me. They were also sorority sisters, mamas, daddies, aunties.

That's when the real nerves kicked in. See, previously, when I performed on these stages in the '80s, people didn't come to see Jenifer Lewis; they came to see my Broadway characters. But now, today, these fans were expecting just me on that stage. Raw and vulnerable and ready to tell the truth. This wasn't Carnegie Hall or Lincoln Center or the big, boisterous venues I was used to. This was a more intimate theater. A place where people would wait in line for an hour just to get a few minutes of me. And maybe afterward, a chance to whisper their life stories in my ear. This was going to be a group therapy session, a moment to get real with my fans, a moment for my fans to get real with me.

But when the lights came on, could I show myself not in character but in my own skin?

I got onstage that night, my script flew out the window. Some woman from the *Huffington Post* or one of those online magazines was sitting up there with me, asking me questions about the book. As a side note: no one should be onstage with me, ever. I'm way too long-winded for that. Give me a mic and get the fuck off the stage! Please.

I lost all the lines I had prepared about my resilience and my overcoming. Instead, I simply looked at the audience and told them my story. They got the whole enchilada, me in all my me-ness. The same girl from Kinloch who had eaten mud pies standing up there on that stage. I talked about my bipolar disorder, my broken engagements, my hopes and dreams, my traumas. I got real about the way I had been molested as a child. I held nothing back. We talked about abortion. The way the world was sick from the huge expectations put on our shoulders. The curtains came and went, and I just stood there on that stage naked.

After I shared the things that had broken my heart, I asked the staff to turn up all of the lights so I could see those beautiful faces in the audience. Then I asked them to turn them down—the people were hideous!!!! I'm kidding. No, I'm not. Okay, seriously, there was so much life behind the eyes of my audience members. Our time together was sacred. I saw the living proof that our secrets connect us. Our secrets heal us.

I did that night after night, city after city, for the next few months. Shed all my cells and was reborn alongside my fans.

Before the book tour, living in a showbiz bubble, I was disconnected from how people were living in the real world. It was nice to be up close again with humanity. It allowed me to see how fragile we are, how sick we are, how angry and abused we are.

My honesty and openness triggered their own righteous truths. The people I met on tour told me their stories about divorces and heartbreak. Stories about health issues and violence. Stories about sexual abuse and mental health and self-worth. Addictions, alcoholism.

The intensity, heaviness, and honesty that filled the auditoriums was absolutely staggering. It was time to change the mood; after all, I'm not a professional therapist. I'm an entertainer. Having done one-woman shows all over the world, I was famous for my ability to turn a room around on a dime. I had to show my ass. I ended the nights telling joke after joke. Hoping my light would seep into the broken parts of their hearts, allowing them to walk in their joy.

The book tour continued. I landed in Philly, where the signing was oversold at the Museum of African American History. They were all so lit up and happy, and I don't know that I had ever felt so loved. The head of the museum asked security to get the benches out of the exhibit rooms to ensure there would be enough seating.

I snuck to the bathroom discreetly, hoping my fans wouldn't charge the stall. But oh hell, if they did, I wouldn't be so mad either. I walked into the restroom, where a stunned and beautiful eighty-year-old woman looked at me as though she had just lost her breath. I slipped into the stall to do my business, and when I came out, there she was, still there, stunning. She walked slowly toward me as I washed my hands. I smiled. As she shuffled over, I held that smile. She came close to me and whispered into my ear: "My husband raped me. They made me marry him. I'm eighty-two. I read your book. I have now left him."

Chills shot down my spine. I held her.

My work allowed for us to see one another. Recognize ourselves in one another through our deep admissions of who we truly are and what had happened to us. When I found out I was somebody, I found out you were somebody too. No matter who is doing what, we are all the same. I was hungry to tell them something I wish I'd known: "Even in your darkest moments, you're already a star. The light is already in ya."

One night, a young, pretty reporter stood up to ask me a question during a press run. She was shaking, nervous, like it was the first question she'd ever asked in her life. "Speak up, little girl," I yelled at her. One thing I'm sure of is that women have no place in keeping quiet. None of us do.

"Miss Lewis, I've heard you say that you like to lead with love. Can you go deeper? What does that look like? What does it look like to actually lead with love?"

"Thank you, sweet pea," I said. I was silent for a moment. *Lead with love*. I had said that line over and over again to audiences everywhere. "I still don't know what it means, but let me try. If you lead with love, you can change your world. Leading with love starts within us. We have to honor ourselves in order to lead. That is the first part of leading with love. The next part is holding the people around us accountable. To lead with love, you have to lose judgment and listen. Listen to yourself. Listen to the people around you. Listen to what the gods have asked you to show up as in this one fantastic life. Just sit down somewhere, be still, and listen."

The book tour and personal growth and amazement in my audience stretched over several months. When we arrived in Fort Lauderdale, Florida, I did a few book signings and visited a few churches before going down to speak with the Parkland high school students. Wherever we were booked, I wanted to know where the horror was, how I could help. A few weeks before I arrived, nineteen-year-old Nikolas Cruz had opened fire on students and staff at Marjory Stoneman Douglas High School. He killed seventeen people and left seventeen more wounded. This killing spree was the deadliest high school shooting in US history. Those Parkland teens had just been through hell. I saw the footage of them all running with their hands above their heads, petrified that they might be shot.

When I visited with the teenagers, I explained that I'd had a knife held to my throat and knew what it was like to be traumatized and to be in utter shock. I know what it's like to feel empty after an event that will forever leave a dark stain on your life. I specifically reached out to the Black teens of Parkland, the ones who weren't getting any press and were suffering. Yeah, that's right. I said it. The little Black kids. They talked to me about who they were. Where the disparities were in the school. How raw they felt. How scared they felt. How they were tired of running for their lives. Nobody's children should have to run from bullets. Not one more. Not another.

We also made a stop in Flint, Michigan. My book event was held in The Whiting, a two-thousand-seat auditorium at Mott Community College. This was my largest audience on the tour and my favorite stop. The piano in that theater was the grandest thing I've seen to date. The people were buzzing, and I was completely in my element. I was familiar with the Flint water crisis, understanding that after a decision by Governor Rick Snyder to switch the community's drinking water source to the Flint River without properly treating it, thousands of people were poisoned by lead and deadly bacteria. I heard my audience talk about the tragic ways it had affected them. After the show ended, I went down to the Flint River and saw the dirty water with my own eyes. I wanted to learn more. My entire being was arrested at the sight of that water. Governor Snyder, who are you?! Switching those people's drinking water over to this poison gunk shit to save you some dollars. Shame. Do you hear me?! Shame.

I took a separate meeting with members of Water Warriors and listened to their stories. I heard how the dirty water affected every aspect of their lives, from their cognitive behavior to their education to their relationships and their sense of self. I reminded them how essential they are—God gave them a voice and it was their right to use it. This situation made me think how few leaders care about Black people, poor people. Flint and Kinloch are full of life and still somehow are viewed by decision makers only as Black cities. We are left in the dust constantly. Fuck that. I resent all that shit, the way we were and still are so consistently tossed to the side. I saw my face in the babies and the mothers of Flint who had barely been able to take a bath in peace. To this day, Flint ain't fixed. The water crisis is not over. The long-term impact should not be forgotten. It was a disturbing situation in Flint, and I left determined to fight for the residents in any way I could.

TAKE YOUR KNEE
OFF MY NECK

Take your knee and privilege off my neck.

It's time for this entitlement and injustice to get checked.

A reality TV star,

Nobody wants a war.

All hands on deck,

take your knee off my neck.

See, nothing was perfect,

But we have been a nation at peace.

Look at all the hate this administration has unleashed,

200,000 deaths worldwide.

We could have been warned,

But he lied and lied.

All hands on deck.

Take your knee off my neck.

Everybody knows what goes around comes around.

How would you feel if someone you loved was taken down?

America,

Rosa did sit on that bus.

Please don't let them divide us.

All hands on deck.

Get your knee off my neck.

They are protesting all over the world, in fact.

How do you expect us to react?

Coming together at the table

Should be next.

Everyone has to get on deck.

But in the meantime,

Keep your nasty knee

Off our necks.

TO HATE THE TYRANT IS TO BECOME THE TYRANT

I take your race away, and there you are, all strung out. And all you got is your little self, and what is that? What are you without racism? Are you any good? Are you still strong? Are you still smart? Do you still like yourself? . . . If you can only be tall because somebody is on their knees, then you have a serious problem. And my feeling is that white people have a very, very serious problem, and they should start thinking about what they can do about it. Take me out of it.

—Toni Morrison, from a 1993 interview

I ONCE HAD A BOYFRIEND named Jeffrey. He was a lawyer. Emotionless but intellectually stimulating. Jeffrey was severely damaged by his mother and had no warmth in his soul. He had herpes, then again so did I, but I liked him because he was tall and sexy, and let me tell you, honey, could he put it down. Back then I had a short fuse, so obviously it was just a hop, skip, and a jump before I wanted to leave his ass. I stayed with him for as long as I could, but his passive nature was starting to get under my skin. I was tired of waking up in the morning and feeling nothing. I was a firecracker, I needed passion, and Jeffrey, well, he was passionless. I was about thirty-two years old, and I sho' didn't have time for the bullshit. I decided I was way too hot to be hopping around Los Angeles with some boring-ass man.

The day I walked into his apartment to deliver him the news that it was over, I wore red heels and a tiny black dress. He was standing there in his boxers and oversize white tee holding a beer at twelve noon. That was another thing I couldn't stand about him, the way he always looked pathetic. When he wasn't working, he was sitting on the couch staring off into space or trying to get into my jeans. He offered me a glass of wine. I declined.

"Baby, I gotta go," I said.

"Where you goin', Jenifer?" he said back.

"No, nigga, I gotta *go go*. It's over."

I saw tears well up in his eyes before he went ahead and swallowed them down. He puffed out his chest real big and began to put up a fight. He didn't want me to go. I told him that I wasn't surprised he was begging but also that's the way it works during a breakup. One person wants to stay and the other person wants to go. I pretty much felt nothing. I was so tired of looking at snot running down his face. I moved toward the door and put my hands up in the air as if to say, *Talk to these*. As I reached for the door-knob, Jeffrey swooped in front of me and planted himself firmly in front of it.

"You're not going anywhere, Jenifer. I'm not letting you leave. Sit down."

Sit down. Those two words were my childhood trigger. Being the youngest child, I was told to sit down my whole life. I was constantly being dismissed and asked to make myself smaller to make less confident people in the room more comfortable. I immediately started seeing red.

"The hell I'm not," I shouted back. "Get the fuck up out my way, Jeffrey. This shit is OVER!"

He doubled down, throwing himself spread-eagle across the door. The biggest mistake he ever made was to look me in the eye and let me know he had a plan to keep me captive. Now, y'all know even back then I didn't want nobody fucking with me in these streets. My screams were so loud that the entirety of Los Angeles County woke up. My voice has always been my greatest weapon.

"HELPPPPPPPPP!" I screamed as he moved toward me, peeling himself away from the door. At that age, my voice could pierce the walls. My vocal cords were meteoric. "LET ME THE FUCK OUTTA HERE, JEFFREY!" I exclaimed, warning him he was in for trouble. "BACK UP, LAWYER BOY!" He took a step toward me. Now, listen. I know this nigga was not about to hurt me, but my rage and disdain for him was uncontrollable, so I popped him right in the face. I was still doing Jane Fonda's workout, bitch. So I knocked him to the floor. I saw red, and *ding, ding, ding,* I won the match. When Jeffrey stood up, he was missing a tooth. He was bleeding from his nose. The left side of his face was completely altered.

I walked out the door, got into my Mazda 323, and drove away. In my rearview mirror, I saw a police car rolling up to Jeffrey's driveway. Po' bastid.

In my early life, rage was my ruler. For as long as I can remember, it has run through my veins. Before my bipolar disorder was treated, this is what my rage looked like: violent, illogical, completely out of control. I could go from zero to two thousand in less than five seconds. I wish that I'd never learned rage and that I was the auntie y'all make me out to be 100 percent of the time, but the truth is, in those days I was bitter with a little bit of sweet sauce on the side.

In my younger years, my rage was out of the ordinary. I mean, sure I popped Jeffrey in the mouth, but I also regularly spent my time ripping T-shirts off the muscular backs of all my boyfriends for any little thing they said to me. Stay in line, mothaFucka! I really did always think it was justified. At the time, I had normalized the rage in my brain. My untreated ass thought nothing was wrong with popping my boyfriend right in the mouth and then driving away, leaving him to deal with Five-O all by his lonesome.

When I trace my rage back, I can see so clearly that it stemmed from my relationship with my mother. Yeah, that's right, I 'm about to blame my hysteria and bad behavior on my mama. Oh, you know it's true—everything stems from our childhood. I know my mother loved me, but never in a way that I could understand. Though she did her best, I felt neglected. And oh my God, the constant ridicule from her. It was ever present. When I was molested as a child, I told my mother and it was ignored. She swept it right under the rug. My mother's indifference toward me shaped my entire understanding of myself. I painted so much of my pain as rage instead of being up front about my hurt. As a result, I spent my teenage years lashing out, starving for attention and then kicking myself when I got it. I built a house made of steel around my body so no one could ever tear me down. I had a deep fear that to lose my anger meant to invite weakness in to replace it. I got into the horrible habit of walking through the world thinking I was protected by armor so thick that nothing could get in. Unfortunately, nothing could get out either. Sure, songs of hope escaped every once in a while, because of my dream, but the truth is, I was always hot under the collar about something. My rage was an addictive cycle that hid me from my constant discomfort.

I believe we all have rage. Whether it's the tiniest bit or a whole scoop of it. I first came to terms with my rage in my midthirties in a session with my longtime therapist Rachel. She always did the good and necessary job of holding a mirror up to my soul. She empowered me to be forgiving. My rage did not have to be my fuel. I practiced, practiced, and fucking practiced setting it down, letting my joy get in on the fun more and more.

Y'all, the pain never goes away, but after years of working

through it—and I mean *working through*—it does dissipate. I learned to check my rage at the door. I worked hard to pull my pain out by the root. At the time I was in therapy, I was 90 percent rage and 10 percent joy, but I learned how to use the tools that allowed me to let that joy shine through.

Tool 1: When I began to feel my rage bubbling up, instead of forcing my way in front of it, I would stop, observe, and breathe.

Tool 2: I would sit in my discomfort, feeling all my feelings, meditating, and journaling about my experience.

Tool 3: I would transform that hot rage into productive action and do my best to lead with love.

Tool 4: Get the fuck up and live.

One morning in early January 2021, I woke up in a funk. There was something in the air. My rage signals began to pop up. I was dizzy with a hot head. I was crawling out of my skin.

I immediately reached for my therapy tools. I canceled all my meetings to protect both myself and the people around me from my rage. I stripped down naked, drew a bath, and stared at the water as it filled up the tub. I dipped one toe in the scalding-hot water and closed my eyes. Then my entire foot followed, as I was interrupted by my phone buzzing next to me. It was my manager. I knew she'd wring my neck if I screened her call after canceling a jam-packed day of meetings, so against my better judgment, I answered.

"Nigga, nigga, nigga, nigga!" I said. Our usual greeting. She never liked that, but she indulged my crazy ass.

"Jen, put on the news right now. It's war." Her voice was sterile. As sharp as a knife. I knew from her tone that she wasn't playing.

The last time I'd heard a tone like that—so desperate, so succinct, so entrenched in trauma—was on September 11, 2001. My boyfriend had called me that morning and said that same thing. He warned me to turn on the news. I remember popping up and turning it on and immediately seeing the smoke filling the entirety of New York City. A city I loved. A city that had taught me how to be. Dear God, nothing would ever be the same. Shockingly, the Twin Towers were on fire. The city was in a panic. The screen was populated with people covered in soot running for their lives and pointing to the sky in horror. What we saw that day was years of untended rage taken out on thousands of innocent New Yorkers.

I hung up the phone and dipped my other foot into the hot bath. If this morning was going to be anything like the morning of 9/11, then I knew I had to do at least one thing for myself to mask the rage I might feel when I turned on the television.

I stayed in the tub until I pruned up. I thought about everything

I might see when I finally did click on the television. I unplugged the bath and dried myself off. I pressed the power button on my remote control. There it was on TV. The rage of a nation. The war we had been anticipating for the past four years was playing out before my eyes.

It was January 6, 2021. The United States Capitol building was being attacked by a mob of Trump supporters. Those roaches stormed the Capitol, y'all. It was an all-out siege. And all the while the gluttonous, narcissistic Orange Man sat on his ass watching TV and eating McDonald's. That orange awful idiot had convinced so many people that there was an America to make great again, he had brainwashed his supporters so deeply, that they went to DC and burned the little bit of respect we had left to the ground.

I watched the way insurrectionists ran toward the Capitol building in disgust. *Is this shit really happening?* We had been storming the Capitol for some time already, disrespecting its very values when we elected a man who poked fun at the handicapped and coined the phrase "Grab 'em by the pussy." *Dear God, what will it take for us to stop?*

The events of the day brought me back to my darkest moments, full of uncontrollable anger so strong it swallowed me whole.

The rage we witnessed on January 6th was a rage that had been bubbling under the surface for generations. These assholes feel entitled to power. Make no mistake: this is what white rage is made of, the constant need to feel powerful. This was unleashed madness. A rage unwarranted. A rage rooted in the abuse of Black

Me with a plate and a pig
promoting my first book,
The Mother of Black Hollywood.

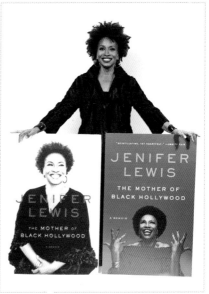

I'm so proud of my memoir.

Me and me.

My life is so damn full.
From left to right:
Pacific Clinics Champion of
Mental Health
Essence: Black Women in Hollywood
I Rise: The Boris Lawrence Henson
Foundation
CARRY (Coalition for At-Risk-
Restoring Youth) The Orchid Award

A night at the Oscars with my baby boy DJ Pierce aka Shangela.

Rehearsing with the great Dolly Parton for Netflix's *Christmas on the Square*.

Me with my baby Lena Waithe— The Queen of Black Hollywood.

My dear friend Laurie Petok. An absolute lifesaver.

Black folks are so proud of me.

My precious siblings. (*From left to right*) Edward Jr., Vertrella, Robin, Jackie, Wilatrel, and Larry Lewis. And I'm the baby, sitting on my big sister's lap!

Kinloch High School. Shoulders back, titties first.

Ready. Set. Action! Po'bastid.

My family that gave me great comfort during the pandemic: (*left to right*) Michiko, Micah, Elijah, me, Isamu, Benjamin, and Jason.

Badass in balloons,
circa 1976.

I understood
the assignment.

Standing before grace, beauty, majesty, and hope. First Lady Michelle Obama.

"Patience" the tiger giving me courage. Necklace adorned by the Maasai tribe in Tanzania.

Sailing to Komodo Island.   Another failed marriage.

In these Havana, Cuba, streets.

This was NOT a nude beach. I was NOT yet medicated. Saint Martin, 1991.

Who let me loose in Antarctica? I almost stepped on this 4-ton smiling elephant seal.

Good Trouble. Me and John Lewis at Tyler Perry's second studio opening.

An early campaign rally with Senator Kamala Harris, now Vice President Kamala Harris.

Supporting CARRY (Coalition for At-Risk-Restoring Youth), with founder Dr. Pearl Grimes (*far right*).

Los Angeles LGBT Center's 50th Anniversary. Warriors for the cause: (*left to right*) me, Lily Tomlin, Jane Fonda, and Kathy Griffin.

With Kendrick Johnson's parents: (*left to right*) Jackie Johnson, me, Kenneth Sr., and Jason Pollock, director of the documentary *Finding Kendrick Johnson*.

Showing support for Colin Kaepernick by wearing Nike on the red carpet at the Emmys.

The Women's March in Los Angeles, January 2020. So very proud of these young ladies.

GET YOUR KNEE OFF MY NECK in the name of George Floyd.

Mama Odie in *The Princess and the Frog*.

Flo in *Cars 1, 2,* and *3*.

Aunt Tallulah in *Tuca & Bertie*.

Miss Patty from *The Ghost and Molly McGee*.

Professor Granville in *Big Hero 6*.

Wheezelene in *Mickey Mouse Funhouse*.

With Molly Shannon and Vanessa Bayer in my new show, *I Love That For You*. I'm having a fucking blast in the role of Patricia.

Bright colors bring me so much joy. Standing in front of my friend Synthia SAINT JAMES's art piece, *Steppin*.

Sitting in front of *Sugar Baby*, a painting by eleven-year-old Helen Leon.

My longtime friend Thom Fennessey backstage at Lincoln Center.

The Wakanda-themed party on the Tom Joyner cruise during my book tour.

Funny-ass Kathy Griffin.

Hanging out with my
Uzbekistan posse.

Gittin' in and gittin' out of Gitgit
Waterfall, Indonesia. Git it?

Antarctica—
CLIMATE CHANGE IS REAL.

Found some
friends in
Singapore.

We made history, y'all. And it was my absolute pleasure.

and brown people. And Asians. Jews. The LGBTQ+ community. Anyone who does not think the way they do. I was horrified, but I'd be damned if I said I was surprised.

White people in this country and across the globe have gotten everything they have ever wanted and more off the labor of Black people. There are untold thousands of people who have been raped, pillaged, and terrorized by white men with whips and guns assisted by their women. White people have flown drugs into disenfranchised communities for decades. Y'all know I could go on and on and on about this. They've planted guns and violence and hate all around us. They created Blackness so they could put whiteness on a pedestal. And as the great Toni Morrison said, "What are you without racism? Are you any good? . . . Do you still like yourself?"

January 6th went down because in this country, they believe that the very concept of whiteness is at risk.

Let's think about it: *Who is really entitled to the rage against this nation?* It certainly wasn't those dumb fucks. This white rage is insulting. The rage of this nation belongs to the marginalized. America's rage belongs to the families of Breonna Taylor and Ahmaud Arbery. It belongs to Gianna Floyd, George Floyd's daughter. It belongs to Kendrick Johnson's parents, Jackie and Kenneth Johnson.

As I stood there, frozen with these thoughts running through my mind, I couldn't help but go back to the first time I'd heard Kendrick Johnson's name. His story warranted the highest rage.

I first heard about Kendrick Johnson when I received a call from a young man named Jason Pollock. He'd seen me perform "Take Your Knee off My Neck" on CNN and asked me to participate in a documentary he was making. "You're the only person who can do this. We need your passion, Jenifer," he said.

It is traditional in our country to dispose of Black children like garbage. On January 11, 2013, the body of Kendrick Johnson was discovered inside a vertical rolled-up mat in the gymnasium of Lowndes High School in Valdosta, Georgia. A preliminary investigation and autopsy concluded that Johnson's death had been accidental; however, his family knew better. The Johnsons had a private pathologist conduct a second autopsy, which, not at all shockingly, concluded that he died from blunt-force trauma. Murdered. When they exhumed the body, they found his insides stuffed with paper. Can you believe the coroner had removed and carelessly discarded Kendrick's organs? Too many people are cruel and heartless.

On October 31, 2013, the US attorney for the Middle District of Georgia announced that his office would open a formal review of Johnson's death. On June 20, 2016, the Department of Justice announced that it would not be filing any criminal charges related to Johnson's death. The Johnson family filed a $100 million civil lawsuit against thirty-eight individuals, alleging that his death was a homicide and that the respondents were participants in a conspiracy that involved the sons of then FBI agent Rick Bell. To no one's surprise, the Johnsons lost their lawsuit and Georgia judge Richard

Porter ordered them to pay more than $292,000 in legal fees to the defendants, accusing them of fabricating evidence to support their claims. The Johnsons were penalized for seeking justice.

Once the fuck again, America has caused severe trauma in the lives of another Black family. Kendrick's life of light would be erased if we let it. Make no mistake, that won't happen on my watch.

America's rage belongs to us who are victimized by systemic racism, not the white people who showed up at the Capitol that day. Now, listen. Everyone knows that I love everyone on this planet. Even the assholes. It don't matter to me what color you are. But when people morph into roaches, showing the worst sides of humanity, the way all those people did that day, smearing shit all over the walls, a bitch needs to be spanked, and trust that I'm the auntie to do it. Despite the blood boiling through my veins that day, I summoned the spirit of Nelson Mandela to lift me up. I visualized the way he walked out of that prison after twenty-seven years and into his freedom, determined to bring enlightenment to everyone. I was inspired by the way he moved forward, lighter, less weighty, more aligned with the good he wanted to put into this world. From that place of peace, he became the leader the world so desperately needed. He led by example. He led with love. Nelson Mandela has been cited as saying words that ring true for me: "Resentment is like drinking poison and then hoping it will kill your enemies." As it turns out, the same logic applies to rage. To hate the tyrant is to become the tyrant. God help me.

I looked around at my home. Where my four little grand-nephews (who were staying with me at the time) were usually cackling. It was silent. These selfish Trump idiots had snatched the joy from children who were usually loudly playing with their new Christmas presents. I wondered when society would move my sweet nephews from cute to threatening? When would they be hunted by these same white men I witnessed on the street? When would these roaches come for them? These little boys— their precious high-pitched voices usually echoing through the halls, running down the stairs every morning, and half drowning my old ass in the pool with their shenanigans—would soon become Black men.

I was scared of what would happen to this country if we continued our great divide. I feared that one day my five-year-old niece who lives down south would be drowning in the waters of a Category 5 hurricane, and that old white man living across the street wearing a MAGA hat, using a Confederate flag as a raincoat, would not save her. I was scared that he would look at her blue lips and say, "Let's get back to the house. That's just one less nigger baby."

I was scared, the way I had been as a child, so I put on my armor. This new armor was even shinier than the armor I wore as a child. This armor allowed me to be both scared and unafraid. The blood in my veins ran so hot and so fast that I barely knew what to do with it.

I thought about the ways this cancer of hatred grows inside of

WALKING IN MY JOY

us. Who is most responsible for it? The Karens and the Kanyes of the world, who seem to be in so much pain that they have to spew their shit all over this country. I'm not one to point fingers, y'all, but today I'm pointing. White women voted for Donald Trump in 2016 and again in 2020. They have deemed themselves the gatekeepers of racism. For centuries they have protected white supremacy and patriarchy with their votes and actions. They've watched their men walk out the door with their white hoods on and they've kept their dinners warm, anxiously awaiting their return. And don't get me started on Kanye West. This mothaFucka led Black people to believe that with Trump in office we might have a fighting chance. After all those kids bought your records—your stupid ass couldn't even give back to 'em. Kanye West, you're a coward. If I ever see you in these streets, just know that Auntie's getting ready to rip you a new asshole. I'm tired of you. Take your medication, little boy. Yeah, I said it.

After I clicked off the television, I biked down to the coffee roasters to get myself a cup of joy. When in doubt, ride it out. As I zoomed down Ventura Boulevard, I saw a short white man standing in front of the coffee shop in that distinct red hat. You know the one. That disgusting Donald Trump MAGA hat that haunted us for years showed up right here in Sherman Oaks. *Aw shit*, I thought. *This mofo is going down.* I pumped the pedals. He had a big ol' smile on his face. Almost celebrating the way our nation's

Capitol was burning at that very moment. That little mothaFucka's hate had come out to play. Unfortunately for him, he would meet his match. I, the alpha wolf, landed directly in front of him with a precise screech of rage in my back tire. I'm surgical with a bike, y'all.

Through gritted teeth, I looked at him and said, "What the fuck is wrong with you?! Your hate is teaching the next generation of children to hate, mothaFucka."

He looked me back in my eye and, with that same rage of the roaches climbing the Capitol walls, said, "Fuck you."

Without pause or hesitation, I whipped back the handlebars like an equestrian, yanking the bicycle from between my legs. Knowing just how close I could get without it being an assault. The front wheel was centimeters from his face. I'm a fool but not a damn fool. I got too much money to be sued for hitting a bitch. Besides, I'm too old for that physical shit, but, oh, thank God for freedom of speech. I screamed, "NO, FUCK YOU!"

He didn't expect such a big voice from such a tiny woman. He was visibly shaken. "You're fucking crazy!!!" he shouted back at me.

Still gritting my teeth, I said, "Yes, little nasty man, I am crazy, so you might want to get the fuck off this corner in that silly-ass hat."

He walked away, chest still puffed to the sky.

I looked around and spotted a young twenty-something girl sitting in a chair sobbing. Terrified of the man. Terrified of me. Terrified of the scene. I walked over to her, reaching my arms out to hold her. She shrank away from me. I felt shame creep up from deep inside my soul. My personality had broken through the medication. I wept with the young girl on the street. I held her hand as I apologized for the war I had just taken part in. At that moment I had become the oppressor, no longer able to judge a gotdamn thing those roaches were doing. I had stooped down to their level.

If I'm honest with myself, my rage was a long time coming. I had been carrying around outrage for quite some time. I was ready to burst. Ready for war. Since 2016 and the election of the Orange Man, my rage had been bubbling up under the surface. Early on in his presidency, I remember seeing a white woman screaming at protestors, "I'm gonna teach my grandchildren to hate you!"

There is so much danger in this battle cry. Hate is the root evil of all disease. It crawls under the skin, and Good Lord, I was far too familiar with it. My explosion had been inevitable. My anger had been manifesting inside me longer than I had realized. It had seeped into my soul, and instead of summoning the best version of myself, I had acted it out. *My shrink is going to kill me.*

A few years before, I had found myself on a slow boat headed to some island off the coast of Singapore. I was traveling, doing one of those solo trips I keep going on about. I felt happy, or at least I was doing my best at being happy on my way to happy. I sat there, taking in the sun and the wind and the earthly smells of Singapore. Hoping that when I got back to the States I'd continue to find the strength to fight the good fight. And be a good girl doing it. As I looked up, I saw a white couple sitting across from me looking my way and whispering to each other. It made me feel on edge. Guarded. They approached me, and all my spidey senses started tingling. There had been so much division that I had begun to combine white people with drama. I was ready to fight. Before they could open their mouths, I calmly looked up and said, "Please don't come over here talking about all your guilty feelings. Y'all are probably some Trump voters. I don't have time to talk about why you believe those kids should be in cages." The pain I saw in their eyes was enormous. The white woman fell silent. She was hurt. She looked at me and said in a low and steady voice, "Don't you dare." The couple walked away. My mind began to race. Shame washed over me. I was so embarrassed and sickened by my actions. When we exited the boat, I searched for them. I wanted to apologize. One of my biggest regrets is that I never found them. A missed opportunity for conversation. Hate is a cycle, y'all. Someone gave it to me and then I gave it to them. It was time to cut it off at the root or it would surely eat me alive.

All of us have walked around with some kind of rage inside of us. The atrocities of the people who bought and sold us, raped us in the cotton fields and hung us, suffocated our children, and shot us, to this day go beyond the realm of reason. We're entitled to our rage, y'all. We've been taught it, and we have to let ourselves feel it. At the same time, we have to come to the table, unite, and learn to use it differently now. There's no room left to run around burning the cities we built to the ground because we can't control ourselves. We are not like them. When they go low, we've got to go high. Instead of acting it out, we've got to write out our rage. Feel it all. Find our way. Then lay down our swords and shields. Try our best and do whatever we can to break the addictive rage cycle. We're still too beautiful for this. White, Black, green, we gotta walk the walk of balance and resolve.

We must continue the work. It is not our job to wake people up, but it is our job to stay awake. To stay vigilant. To make sure every one of those mothaFuckas knows we will never quiet down again. The work never stops, my friends. The work is ever present. The work is the only thing we have left.

/ KENDRICK JOHNSON /

Did you call him a nigger before you took his organs out?

Nobody is sitting down for this.

We're gonna stand, scream, and shout.

Because, just like you, we love our children

And the color of their skin.

We're tired of being notified as the next of kin.

Kendrick Johnson was seventeen,

Just starting his young life.

Someone murdered him,

Then they gutted him with a knife.

We've read too many of these stories.

We all know exactly what this is about.

Did you call him a nigger before you took his organs out?

MUD PIES AND THE MAASAI

IF YOU'VE NEVER MADE a mud pie from scratch and then eaten it, do not come for me. You see, I grew up so poor I didn't even know what rich was. I didn't know about glitz, glamour, and fame. It was so far away I couldn't even imagine it. I couldn't see it. I couldn't picture what a nice, comfortable life without any hardship looked like at all. I never really cared about money until I was hungry and there was no food. My reality consisted of low ceilings, bathtubs filled with boiled water, and a cold stove. Lots of siblings piled on top of one another. Little Jenny hiding in a cabinet, terrified that my mama would find me and lay into me the way she always could.

Kinloch trained me to be savvy—I mean it in the fiercest way. Kinloch was simultaneously so mean and so good to me. Home. A whiplash of emotions. Sometimes up and sometimes down but, honey child, always, always, always poor as hell. Yeah, that's right, bitch, I come from the streets and great poverty.

Early on in my life, I learned to run from things that brought me pain. In my twenties and thirties, I ran to New York. When I had reached the highest point in New York, having finished three Broadway shows and touring with Bette Midler, I ran to Los Angeles. I ran and ran and ran. I was unconsciously hiding from the things that hurt me most.

Fortunately, I always met myself where I landed. The same racing of the mind, the same weariness inside my soul, just in a different city. But still, I was convinced that I could get away from myself. If I kept running, I could tell myself any story I wanted to and build a new reality.

After years of therapy, medication, and journaling, things slowed down. I didn't go from Flo-Jo to a turtle, because I knew it took a hundred years for an oak tree to mature and I was willing to take the ride. Breaking habits is a bitch, y'all. Change is just fucking hard.

Doing the work modified my behavior. I slowly but purposefully stopped running from myself long enough to hear my own voice. I listened to myself deeper than before. And let me tell you, I was one scary mothaFucka. I stayed steady for a while, not running. Stable. I threw myself into my career more healthily. I grounded myself in characters not so that I could get away from myself but instead so that I could meet myself in a neutral place.

In 2016, after years and years of treatment, I found myself in a position where I wanted to run again. Shit hit from all sides. When it rains, it pours, but I was a little too waterlogged. Fuck it—I was tired of doing the work. I reverted back to my old ways.

All the stuff that I had combatted finally caught up to me. I had to get away. My best friend had been diagnosed with cancer and it hit me hard. There was something about getting older that hit me. I was realizing the impermanence of life. Swallowing down the idea that I wasn't going to live forever (e.g., telling y'all on *The Breakfast Club* that I only had thirty summers left) and neither were the people I loved. There's something about this idea that I might be running out of time. God had given me so much more than I could have imagined. But this TKO was too much. I couldn't face it. I had to get up and go.

I remembered a party I went to early on in my career somewhere in the Hollywood Hills. I met a white woman with big lips and a face tucked so tightly I could see her bones. The work she'd had done on her face was so obvious that I held my breath the entire time she spoke for fear her skin would burst. But what came from her mouth I never forgot. In a drunken slur, she said, "You wanna go see the face of God, Jen? All right, then go on a safari. We just got back."

At the time, I was thinking, *Bitch, I can't afford nothing like that.* Well, Merry Christmas, bitches—*black-ish* came along, and that's right!!!! I was going to Africa, bitches!!!!!! I thought I could lose myself among the epic nature of it all. I thought I might finally achieve my goal of disappearing into the savanna and the Serengeti.

When I landed at Kilimanjaro International Airport, my only concern was, how in the world did I fuck this up? Now, look: you don't land near Kilimanjaro at night. For God's sake, Jenny, you just don't. You can't see the grandness of Mt. Kilimanjaro at night! You can't see the way it stretches directly to the sky, sun peaking above its flat top, revealing the glory of the cumulonimbus clouds beneath it. I guess I missed the memo, and as a result, boy, did I miss the magic. Like a fool, I was in the back seat of my Range Rover cussing, asking the driver if I would be able to see it coming back. He told me if the clouds allowed for it, then I might just get lucky.

The next morning, my tour guide drove out into a mighty desert. I was so far from home and yet so close to it. We weren't in Kinloch, but, by God, did I understand what it felt like to live in a place that was so barren. I could see, clear as day, even at night, the familiar, sad, unfair, oppressive, ridiculous poverty that exists there. I saw myself in the kids who ran alongside my car, asking for money. There were far too many. I saw myself in them as they walked miles home from the one school available to them, and in the bathtubs full of lukewarm water.

Let me pause here and say that I always nicely ask my travel agent to do her best to hook me up with a handsome, well-informed tour guide with white teeth, and a hot body. Little Jenny Lewis wants only the foiiiiinest of the foine guides. I promise y'all I never touch any of them. Okay, yes, I did. Okay, no, I didn't. Yes, I did. Okay, not on this trip, but ONE TIME I did in a different city. I digress.

As we drove through the desert, I saw sights that I will never forget. There were oxen, big bovine gods, glorious and ginormous, just ahead of us. There were children at play, their Crest-white smiles beaming, the sun reflecting their teeth. My first sighting was the baobab trees. Then the vast landscapes revealed the face of God—nature in its inarguable magnificence. There was no lens powerful enough to capture its brilliance. There were only two words dominating my brain: *Jesus Christ*. I saw Thomson's gazelles, starlings and storks, the mischievous play of baboons, and blue and black birds—everything was so majestic. There were elephants of all sizes, wary of us. One actually came for my ass too. Don't fuck with no elephants, y'all. I even spotted six cheetahs running at high speed with meat dangling from their mouths. I don't know what they caught, but whatever it was, the mothaFucka was dead. Lionesses surrounded our jeep. I, of course, named them all after my cousins; Joy, Jada, Justine, Jocelyn, Jasmine, Jojo, and of course Keisha, Shaniqua, and Laquanda.

There are no words, ladies and gentlemen, for the moment you find yourself face-to-face with a creature as godly as a lion. Let me tell you, if you can *ever* go on a safari, do, but you might want to wear Depends. The rhinos were bigger than my house. The hyenas were cackling, the giraffes had their heads up in the clouds. The wildebeests were slurping down their breakfast at the watering hole. Every zebra's coat glistened distinctly under the sun. These animals were the paintings of God. Every bit of them was intentionally made. Too magnificent and powerful for words.

As we approached my cabin at the resort near Tarangire National Park, we came upon a landing of golden grass. In all this golden grass, I spotted a bright red color. A color so regal, so grand, so unlike any tone I'd ever laid my eyes on before. What could be so red in the middle of all of this? Was it a bird? A rare animal? Blood from a gazelle leftover from a hungry lion? As the red began to move through the golden blades, I recognized that what I had laid my eyes on was in fact the blanket of a Maasai warrior. My Maasai warrior. The Maasai are a people who have kept their sacred traditions intact through all the ups and downs of the continent. Through all the invasions and madness of white men raping its resources, they have prevailed. They are larger than life in their values. Humble and fierce. True warriors at heart.

My guide parked the jeep, and a short little Maasai warrior greeted me. *What the fuck? Where the hell is the TALL, GODLY MAASAI WARRIOR I was promised?! That's the one I wanted!* As he escorted me to my cabin, he pointed out the hippopotamus pond. Can you believe my life? Boy, have I lived. A hippopotamus pond. I was happy it was about ninety feet away because the stench of those four-thousand-pound, wondrous, ugly fuckers was mighty funky. But I smiled at this beautiful man and politely said, "Yes, the hippo pond is fabulous, shorty."

I later found out these breathtaking warriors had been hired as security for these cabins that sit out in the middle of the plains. As we walked down the dirt road toward my cabin, my knee began to hurt from all the flying, hiking, and long drives. Age again. I heard

Dr. Yun's voice, talking about the "falling years," and looked down at my feet as they navigated the road. This walk was just far too long. *What if I was an obese American tourist who had to walk damn near a mile to a cabin?!* I mean, after all, these eight-star tent-shaped cabins had been built for the rich and elite. And y'all know the rich and elite don't play when it comes to their fitness. Unless of course you're Orange. When we reached my cabin, I took my shoes off and passed out immediately, face first, on the deluxe pillows of my California king-size bed smack dab in the middle of the Motherland.

We had been told there would be a night tour, because most of the animals come out at night, in part to escape the heat of day. But it rained and rained as only it could rain in this ancient land. I chased the rains down in Africa, if only I could just take some of this rain back to dry-ass California. I skipped the tour and dinner because I knew I had to wake up at 3:00 a.m., to be ready by 3:30 a.m. to be driven about forty miles in an old jeep that would take me to a hot-air balloon, to witness the sun rise over the Serengeti. That's not a sentence you hear every day, bitches.

And sure enough, at 3:30 a.m. sharp there was a soft knock on my door. I opened it, and THANK GOD, HALLELUJAH, there stood my ten-foot king. Truly this was a gorgeous, stunning, magnificent Maasai mothaFucka of the mothaFuckas coming to pick me up. Hold me down, Black Jesus. Y'all know where my mind goes when I see a ten-foot man in front of me! I was amazed, humbled, and turned on at the same time. He stood like the Matterhorn, cloaked in a red and blue shuka blanket, beaded from head to toe. His hair braided and locked in dry and unpolluted mud. He carried only a flashlight. He said, "Ready, Mum?" I said, "Yeah, I'm ready, baby, for anything you need me to do." Baby. Only I would call a ten-foot Maasai warrior "baby."

We proceeded to walk to the reception building on this now extremely muddy road. I wasn't much for talking at 3:30 in the morning, but I did mention to him how that heavy rainfall had sounded like a stampede of wild horses I'd seen in Mongolia. He responded with a nod and one word: "Mum." We marched on in a slightly creepy silence. It was all so *Out-of-Africa*-ish. To my surprise, he then turned and said, "Mrs. Charlotte at the front desk tells me you are a famous person, but I knew it too. *The Fresh Will Smith Show*." He'd obviously been watching TV here at the resort because it sure wasn't at the mud-hut village. I blushed and then of course started talking about myself. I mean, what else was I supposed to do?! After all, we had another twenty minutes on this sloshy bitch of a walk.

We bonded as I went on and on and on about me, me, and me. Now, understand, ladies and gentlemen, once again, this is the *Serengeti Plain*. There are no streetlights in these fucking streets. The dark clouds had not yet passed. There was no moon. There were no stars. Pitch-black is an understatement. When I mentioned I was in *The Preacher's Wife,* the Maasai warrior stopped and said, "You were with Whitney Houston?" I was about to say, "Yes, I was, baby. I played her mother!" Just as I took another breath to go on again about *me, me, me, me, me, me, me, me*, we were suddenly interrupted by a rude and heavy crunch.

The king and I both froze as he shined his flashlight quickly in the direction of what was now a louder, too close, mighty crunch. Just when a little pee escaped me, out of the whistling thistle bushes emerged a Cape buffalo. It was huge, jet-black, and not to be fucked with under any circumstances. The light revealed its metallic-like shiny coat, and every thick bulging muscle was defined. I knew it was a female by the shape of her horns. I also knew that if she had a baby buffalo in tow it wouldn't matter if the Maasai man were eighty feet tall or I had done ten thousand movies. We would be two dead mothaFuckas. An article I had read before leaving for the trip claimed, "herbivorous bovines (plant-eating cows) do not eat humans, but they are extremely aggressive and vengeful and will charge if threatened." If that's not proof we sometimes draw our fears to us, then I don't know what is. Another note is the Cape buffalo has been nicknamed "Black Death" by the hideous assholes with small penises who shoot them for sport.

Our heads followed Mrs. Black Death in unison as she slowly proceeded to cross the road in front of us. We could see her one shiny eye. Without words, we both were praying that she would continue on, but of course she stopped, standing just twelve feet from us.

The king tilted his head down at my short ass and out of the side of his mouth, through a small opening of his lips, he whispered, "Don't move, Mum."

Do I look like I'm fucking moving? The only thing that did move was the pee down my safari jeans. At the smell of my pee, she proceeded to whip her head around, pointing her horns directly at us. Both her eyes were lasering in on me and the Maasai warrior, as if to say, "Who y'all?!"

At this point I wanted to approach her and say, "Uh, listen, sistah girl. I'm Jenifer Lewis from St. Louis. I am an award-winning Broadway-Hollywood entertainer. Now, you're Black, I'm Black, and I've got to get back to *black-ish*, so if you don't mind, I'm gonna trudge on through this thick-ass mud with this fine-ass warrior and keep it moving!" But of course none of that happened.

I peeked around the Maasai warrior to see if this bitch was truly about to charge us, because y'all know if that was the case, I was gonna push his tall ass into this bitch's horns and run my ass off. This time in a growling whisper, he firmly instructed me, "Please don't move, Mum." And with those words, this royal man chivalrously and gallantly extended his arms straight out, creating a twelve-foot wingspan with his shuka, and floated it in front of me, making himself bigger than Mrs. Black Death. And so began the standoff. I watched in awe, still slightly peeing myself until sistah girl turned her horns forward and vanished into that wet night.

My poor little heart was pounding harder than ever before. I felt vulnerable, numb, and so scared, but then of course grateful and relieved, all at the same time. I wanted to kill whoever the management of this establishment was for making me feel this unsafe on my vacation.

I imagined my new Maasai assistant saying under his breath, "First-world problems."

Sure, he would be right, but fuck him and y'all too for thinking it. I then looked up and said words to him that no sane human being would ever say to such a divine entity who'd just saved her life. "Nigga . . . get me the fuck outta here."

I proceeded to pound on him, not knowing what else to do. You must understand, when a man is ten feet tall and you're five four, you're pretty much beating his balls. I screamed while boxing his testicles, "What the fuck are you doing out here with these rich-ass white people in the middle of the gotdamn desert? And where the *fuck* is your spear? Every time we see a statue of a Maasai he's got a spear in his hand! I get one with a fucking *flashlight*? Now bring your fine ass on, before a lion rips my face off." He and I laughed all the way to the main building, trying not to remember how close we had come to Mrs. Black Death.

By the way, everybody, I told just a little lie. It wasn't pee—it was poop. Another ass-ident. Yeah, I said it. After having washed my ass in the lobby bathroom and thrown cold water on my face, the driver and I got into the jeep that would take us to where a big bright multicolored hot-air balloon sat at the ready. When he started the engine and turned on the lights of the antiquated vehicle, I immediately understood why I had been detained by the Cape buffalo. If we had not been delayed, I would have missed the wild scene about to unfold. The lights from the jeep captured two adolescent lions, with sweet young manes around their faces.

They were in pounce position, stalking something we could not see. Within a second, we saw a baby wildebeest, legs shaking, in the air. All I could think in my horrified state was, *As amazing as all this shit is, it's fucking scary too. And I wanna go home.* But being the alpha, y'all know I am onward and upward, and upward, and upward.

Less than an hour later, there it was, the rising, raging glory of the flaming majesty we call the sun. No sooner had she finished her silent dance, lo and behold, the herds revealed themselves beneath us. At one point an African harrier-hawk flew by at damn near ninety miles per hour and let out a loud shriek, reminding us this was his territory, not ours.

Just as he shrieked, I felt my stomach turn and the hot-air balloon begin to lose steam. You can't make this shit up, y'all. The propane cylinders started to putter. *Fuck!* The tour was an hour, and we'd only been on this bitch for thirty minutes. The balloon lost its rhythm, and we began to descend, far too quickly, toward the ground. I imagined the headlines: DOUBLE D CUP DIVA GOES DOWN IN THE DESERT. This was one hell of a trip. We crashed. Everyone was safe, but the loud thud and impact gave me one thought and one thought only: *I want to go home.*

There, in that moment, I had the chance to completely forget about the thing I had come running from. Between this shit and the Cape buffalo, the only thing I had time to think about was my breath. Now, snapping back into reality, I thought, *If this is what's in store for me, then I am done running. I'd rather face my realities*

than be hunted by Mrs. Black Death and then free-fall through the
sky with a bunch of white strangers and a Maasai warrior to boot. I
know, you're thinking it again: first-world problems! That night, I
lay awake under the stars, laughing at my unforgettable day: a buffalo, a balloon, and a beautiful Black Maasai man. I could barely
fall asleep at the absurdity of it all.

———

The next day was even more glorious. It was finally time to visit a
village of the Maasai. I packed into a big truck full of other tourists
and we trekked outland to see the culture. When we arrived, I was
adorned with a necklace made of ten trillion beads by an elder
woman. Majestic in her own right, she looked at me, held me, and
whispered, "Welcome home." Our jeep was full of white people,
so y'all know how happy the Maasai people were to see me! A rich
Black woman with red lips. Successful bitches. They immediately
brought the chief's son to meet me. He directed us to the school,
where the kids sang and read in English. It was beautiful. Everything was made of wood. There were no computers. Just books
and the pure air and the earth. Shelves built from trees. These
people were amazing.

When I got a moment, I snuck away from the group and went
into a mud hut where they were cooking goat meat in a lovely
pottery pot above a raging red-hot fire. Of course, me being me,
I asked to taste it. The woman who was cooking gave me a look
and then obliged by slipping a tiny itty-bitty piece of meat into my

hand. I didn't realize this shit was measured for every child to have dinner. I was such an asshole for asking. Just as I was about to put the goat into my mouth, I realized that I hadn't had shots to eat this type of meat in Africa. I became paranoid as hell. *You can't eat their food!* Or maybe I could have and didn't know I could. Either way, I wasn't about to try. I had this little chunk of goat in my hand and I had absolutely no idea what to do with it. Shame on me. I felt like shit. I was ready to throw the meat on the ground, but the ground was so spotless that I couldn't get away with it. I stuck it in my pocket. Now I was freaking out, hoping that a lion wouldn't smell it on our way back to the resort and decide to have me for dinner instead.

When I left the hut, I met back up with my white posse. The Maasai were jumping, performing their ritual dances, and throwing spears for spectacle. It was an unbelievable sight, the way they stood there, jumping like Olympians. Their bodies were slim and tight. As fit as the cheetahs, they could take down a lion themselves.

I spotted the chief's son as he took his turn to throw the spear. His wingspan was wide and broad and unlike anything I'd ever seen. He threw the fuck outta that spear, y'all. Without hesitation, I looked at him and said, "Can I throw it too?!" He looked down, like, *Bitch, are you serious?!* But because they were happy that I was Black, they let me. HA! It's not all bad, y'all. There are perks. As I grabbed the spear, that same elder woman who had adorned me quietly noted that no woman had ever thrown a Maasai spear before. I was honored. I threw that spear and it landed about twenty feet in front of me. Not my best, but then again, not my worst.

What a people these people were. When we got back into the jeep, I waved at the Maasai with a lasting picture in my mind of their beauty. It was as if there were no bipolar meds in me at all. I cried all the way back to my cabin. These were my people. Thank God they didn't steal us all from Africa. These were the survivors.

As I tucked myself in that night, it was becoming clear how far I'd run only to find myself in my place of origin. Every step I took was a step toward myself, not away from me. As I drifted asleep, I saw little Jenny, in Kinloch under those dark skies, dreaming about the life I was living today. In order to move forward, I had to let my lovelessness go. I had to stop running. Let my pain fall away, or at least sit still with it. I closed my eyes with these thoughts and began dreaming.

In my dream, I was a warrior. Half child, half adult. I had been raised as a thief in a tribe on the west plains of Tanzania. I observed myself: a little girl in the jungle taught to be quiet so as not to disturb the hunt. My father was my leader there. He taught me stealth. He taught me survival.

He taught me how to take things—things that I deserved, things that should be mine.

As I watched myself move through the jungle, there was a loud boom. Then I found myself on a slave ship on the Middle Passage. There we all were, stacked together, lying in our shit, helpless. I was chained, confined against the walls with my people and listening to the steps of the white men who had captured us coming down into the hold. They were coming to rape us. I squirmed, searching for my way out as they approached aggressively. One of them, a big man with a belly, held my face, and as he pressed his filthy, spiteful, pink burned skin against mine, I used the stealth my father had taught me to take the gun out of his holster. I slipped his weapon into my hand, and before he could say a word, I killed him. I took his keys and his knife and ran up to the top deck and killed all those white fuckers, like in Nina Simone's version of "Pirate Jenny."

I took a breath, raced down to the hold, pulled the extra-heavy chains from the wrists and ankles of my fellow people. I told them they were free. As gently as I could, I unleashed the bits from their mouths and muscles in atrophy. They looked at me in awe, crawling up the steps to the top deck. Stiffly bent, weary of the restraints, they wept. But then something glorious happened. Their bodies became strong again. Full of life and confidence. One by one, they stood up, heads held high to the sun. They each approached me, held my hands in theirs, and said boldly, "One day I'll have a great-great-great-grandson named John Lewis. One day I'll have a great-great-great-granddaughter named Kamala Harris. Named Stacey Abrams. Named Martin Luther King Jr. Named Malcolm X. Named Tamika Mallory. One day our children will be free again."

Then I woke up.

I was still, stalking the light of every star shining down on me from the skies over the Serengeti. They were brighter now. I was overwhelmed by a peace that surpasses understanding. I was able to see that, even through hardship and pain, I was strong enough to persevere. I was ready to let go and heal my past wounds. Accepting that those things that had broken me had let the light in. I had to forgive myself for running and have the courage to face whatever the waters had to offer next. I had to forgive God for letting all these things happen to little Jenny and the world around me. My dream affirmed that I could call on the ancestors anytime I needed. It was time to be open to life and all the experiences it had to offer. Getting out of my routine had reminded me that life is wondrous no matter where I am. My spirit was invigorated. *Breathe, Jenifer,* I thought. *Don't run.*

On the small plane back to Kilimanjaro from Arusha, I saw the clouds had cleared, and I set my sights on the mountain. My God, my God, my God. A little barefoot colored girl, who'd eaten mud pies for lunch, had now seen the mightiest parts of planet Earth.

Suddenly I no longer wanted to go home. I was home.

/ WE'VE GOT
TO SAVE OUR
CHILDREN /

Women, women, we've got to save our children.

Men, men, you've gotta help us win.

Children are who we're fighting for.

Nobody and nobody wants a civil war.

We cannot divide.

We gotta keep the resistance alive,

Alive, alive, alive, alive.

Women, women, we've got to save our children.

Men, men, you've gotta help us win.

The world is on fire.

When they go low,

We gotta go higher, and higher, and higher, and higher.

Women, women, we've got to save our children.

Men, men, you've gotta help us win.

EPILOGUE

WELL, Y'ALL, A LOT OF shit has happened since I wrote *The Mother of Black Hollywood*. *Black-ish* has ended after eight successful years, and I am starring in *I Love That for You* on Showtime with Vanessa Bayer, Molly Shannon, and an outstanding cast.

I was walking in my joy when I began writing these pages in 2018. Can you believe that I didn't finish until November 2021? Let me tell you, when you think you have a plan, life always seems to get in the way. Or maybe the more appropriate thing to say is that life seems to show you the way. The writing process was challenging, to say the least. But the real challenge is the tough exercise of coming to terms with one's self. I could have retreated into the little Jenny Lewis, full of pain and fear in the fetal position. Or rise up my brown ass and utilize the tools I knew I possessed. After decades of therapy, I chose the latter.

Who you know is Jenifer Lewis, the Queen. Publicly, I am your auntie, yo nigga, your OG Aunt Helen, and of course, let us not forget, the Mother of Black Hollywood. But in these pages I hope you have seen that I am just as human as you are. I laugh. I cry. I get sick. I get my heart broken. And I break people's hearts. I have insecurities and vulnerabilities, and I also fall down so often that my default mode has become the glorious act of getting back up.

So I scrapped all the pages I had written in 2018 and I started fresh. No more pretending. No more acting like I have all the answers when all I really am doing is trusting my gut and putting one foot in front of the other. I found a deep will, courage, and strength to just take one bloody step at a time and unshackle the chains of what became my biggest nightmare: *What right do I have to sit here and tell you to walk in your joy if I'm not doing it?* You never forget bliss once you touch it, and at that moment I had temporary amnesia. It became abundantly clear that I was not allowed to write this book until I became this book.

I have learned it is my job to take care of me and to make sure it is me who wears a smile. I needed to give that gift of laughter to myself. In recent years, I gave that laughter and joy to everyone but myself. I'd dig my heels in, not leaving until everybody was doubled over, laughing so hard they either peed on themselves or eventually waved their arms, pleading with me to shut the fuck up so their stomachs could stop hurting from the cackling. Listen to me: laughter is the greatest healer. Laugh your ass off, even if shit ain't funny. Just laugh, bitch. I thought that if I could put a smile on everyone else's face, then I could save the world. I thought that if everyone else was happy, well then, I had done my job. Boy, was I wrong about that.

While everyone else was laughing, I was not. I just wasn't—not on the inside, anyway. I was stifled by my undiagnosed mental illness. Not knowing I had a disorder, everyone got the chance to experience my joy except me. Once I received help through therapy and medication, I fought for my own happiness every day. I became hell-bent on saving myself. It was an intentional choice, and it wasn't the easy one, but I did it, y'all.

My life has been enriched as a result. Today I'm still a bad mama jama, but I'm also much more intentionally rooted in the bold ways I want to serve the world. My life has become less about me and more about we. And, baby, the WE includes YOU. I care about you.

Hear this, please: You are *not* alone. You are never alone. Look at you. You're with me now. I'm gonna be right here. At this very moment I am reaching both my arms out to you, and with all the wisdom, humanity, and strength I can muster, I am pulling you up. Yeah, that's me, actress, author-activist, greatest entertainer that ever lived, sexy, sassy, ratchet, not-so-bougie movie star, who ain't really got time for your ass. But come here. Get up. I'm gonna hold you and rock you for about ten seconds. Okay, maybe fifteen if you're an asshole and can't let go. Now do me a favor. Go do that for somebody else right now. Call somebody and say, "Yo my nigga, what up? Ha u dern? Have you read Jenifer Lewis's second book? Auntie ain't playin' in this one."

Love you!

Credits and Permissions

All insert photographs courtesy of Jenifer Lewis except as noted below:

Insert, page 12, top right: © Disney/Pixar

Insert, page 12, center right: © Disney Channel

Insert, page 12, bottom right: © Disney Television Animation

Insert, page 13: Jill Greenberg/SHOWTIME

Insert, page 16: ABC / Dario Calmese

Acknowledgments

Natalie Guerrero: I once introduced Natalie Guerrero as my ghostwriter and she corrected me with great conviction to say, "I'm helping her write her book." I was appalled. Bewildered. I thought, *Thiiiiiiiis bitch don't wanna be called a ghostwriter?!* So, ladies and gentlemen, I give you Natalie Guerrero. This young miracle came into my life at a time when I couldn't afford to fall apart but was, indeed, falling fast. You know, COVID bullshit. She bounced up my stairs with them little click-click shoes on August 9 in a mini-skirt I hadn't seen since 1960. She was not only a tiny twig of a girl but also dressed like Twiggy. From how well educated and put together she was, I knew instantly she had been loved as a child. I thought, *Oh shit. This little millennial won't last a day in a room with me.* She was far too sweet and precious.

I gave her a tour of my home because I wanted her to know what she was getting into. I showed her every single one of my trinkets and collectible items from all over the world, flinging all my life stories in her direction. Attempting to scare her away. As much as I tried, little Natalie didn't flinch. Long story short, ladies and gentlemen, this little bunny came in here and turned into a Tyrannosaurus rex. She helped me write the shit outta this book. But what blew me away more than anything was her joy. Whatever breakdown I was having on any given day, Natalie held space for it. When I'd look up after melting down, threatening to throw the entire manuscript in the pool, she'd look back at me with the most captivating smile and, without a word, would convince me to begin again. I knew what she was thinking: *Po'bastid.*

Natalie's writing skills are ferocious. I would say some shit, and within ten seconds of her fingers on the keyboard, it was poetry. That smile of hers never went away. There was an immediate connection between Natalie and I. Boundaries never had to be set because we spent our time writing this book laughing our fucking asses off. Yeah, that little smile got on my nerves a lot when I had to dive headfirst into the woes of my life to churn out these pages, but if it were not for that smile and the pure love she has for writing, read my lips: this book would have never happened. Ladies and gentlemen, boys and girls, I'm happy to announce that Natalie did survive our time together. She's alive and thriving in Los Angeles. What a feat. Four months in a room with Auntie constantly trying to wipe that silly smile off her face so she'd know life wasn't all clacky shoes, miniskirts, and happy-happy.

Natalie, I just have three words for you: YAZZZZZ. WRITE. BITCH.

ACKNOWLEDGMENTS

Tracy Sherrod: I love you. Thank you for trusting me to write another book and for pushing me and Natalie. It's your smile and your laugh and your insane intelligence that moves me more than anything. I would not have written this book if you and only you had not asked. Butters sends a kiss.

Laurie Petok: Laurie One Pot of Chili, Laurie a Ming Lo, Laurie Winky, Laurie the Planet Mercury Is Not in Retrograde Today. You are a gotdamn national hero because you saved a national treasure. Thank you for being an adult and setting boundaries. Thank you for the plants, the food, the flowers, trees, your ridiculous, insane sense of humor and comedic timing. Special thanks to your family: Michael, Marla, Jack and Eli, Frannie, and Nick, aka Milky Way. Bitch, you've done nothing.

Mel Berger: What a champion you are. You stepped in and saved everything. Thank you, Mel.

My *black-ish* cast: Wow. What a ride we've been on together. We walked onto the Disney lot eight years ago as colleagues and we left as a family. The last day on set I rode around the Disney lot like a kid on my little red cruiser and it was a true trip down memory lane. In my head, I saw the squirrels that Butters ran too fast toward, resulting in him breaking his back leg. I remembered the glorious conversations we had, Michelle Obama visiting us on set, the way I crashed Simone Biles's trailer, the Halloween parties, the babies that were born, the marriages, and the Christmases we shared will be etched in my brain for years to come. We lived so much life alongside one another. Yara, Marcus, Marsai, and Miles, y'all are ever beautiful. My TV grandbabies. So proud of you. Tracee, I will miss you calling me Jenny. Anthony, I will miss you calling me crazy. Laurence, I will miss you calling me the baddest bitch that ever lived. I love you all. Onward and upward.

Mark Alton Brown: There are no words. None. We've known each other 693 years and we're still alive. I love you, Bobby, Ella, and Sander. You are my family.

DJ Pierce, aka Shangela: My brother, son, friend, cousin, sister, niece, and main Negro. I'm insanely proud of you. Ten years you lived in my basement; ten thousand years you'll live in my heart.

Nerses Nick MateVosian: Li'l boy, there's so much love in you that it's crazy. Thank you for assisting me in my wonderfully insane life. "Dumbass. I'm taking the dog."

Darren Jones: Auntie loves you and is oh so proud of you. Thank you so very much for helping me with this book.

Kathy Griffin: Just don't chop my head off, bitch. I love you. I want to thank you for sharing your pain with the world. It makes us all feel less alone.

Jonathan Howard: There are no words for how you've taken care of me these many years. My agent, my brother, and my amazing friend. By the way y'all, this ain't the same Jonathan that was useless in Dumbass Nancy.

Freya: Hello, sunshine. I wouldn't be alive had I never met you.

Butters Lewis: ehshahsamunananaynananay dusuno.

Jason Rice: Thank you for keeping me healthy and safe during COVID.

Michiko Rice: There are no words for your kindness. Not to mention beating me down while training me.

The Rice brothers—Micah, Benjamin, Isamu, and Elijah: Auntie is just so proud of all of you. You are the champions of my heart. T-Janie loves you.

Brandy Norwood: Brandy, Brandy, Brandy. Li'l Brandy. All I can say is, Auntie loves you to the moon, baby. To the sun and stars. You are truly the vocal bible, and I'm so very proud of you.

The Coffee Roaster team: Thanks for loving me so damn much. Love all y'all Black. Thanks for writing "Jenifer MF-ing Lewis" on my coffee cup every morning.

Marc Shaiman: Seven-time Oscar nominee. Emmy, Tony, and Grammy winner. One of the most talented lunatics I know. This po'bastid thinks he's my best friend. I love you, pumpkin.

Nita Whitaker: The sweetest, most joyful person I've ever known. You actually get on my nerves. Sing out, baby. And give Scott, Skye, and Liisi some sugar for me.

Bette Midler: You recognized my talent and hot messiness. Then you taught me how to survive in it. Love ya to the moon. All hail the queen.

Roxanne Reese: What's it been, forty-five years? That's over a billion seconds of love.

Terry Burrell: For always being there, laughing your ass off and lifting us all up. I love you, your amazing singing voice, and your believing in me.

Lon Hoyt: You know what bone I'm talking about.

Sharon Stone: You gave me everything off camera. I learned that day.

Allee Willis: My baby girl who would ALWAYS bring the party, the art, and laughter. I miss you so much. RIP Sweetie.

Michelle Obama: For gracing the *black-ish* set and for gracing the world.

C. J. Emmons: For *The Mother of Black Hollywood* song. You know you saaaaaaang, baby boy.

Lance Williams: For the GREAT massages and even better friendship.

Rose Wilson: Since high school, we're still here laughing and acting a damn fool. I love you, Rose.

Clare Bathé-Williams: You think about me every day. I think about you every day. There is no measure to how much I love you. Sang, baby, sang.

Dolly Parton: Pardon me, Dolly. I had a great time working with you. I knew you could sing, I knew you could act, but I didn't know you were so damn funny. I had a blast. Love you. Oh, and when you sang "Happy Birthday" to me, I played it over ten zillion times.

Debbie Allen: If you ask me to put a mouse costume on again, it's gonna be me and you on the dance floor, you little slut. "Who you calling little?!" Dance, baby. Dance.

Debra Brown: For Ruby Johnson's hair and laughing at every damn thing I say.

Devetta McIntyre: For the Microsoft museum honor.

Whoopi Goldberg: Nu Mu. I love you.

Tyler Perry: Thanks for loving me so damn much. BLACKATCHA, BROTHER! So DAMN proud of you.

Taraji P. Henson: You already know. Lots of kisses, boo.

Tim Curtis: Thank you for all the animations, commercials, and love. Love you, Black baby boy.

The people of Kinloch, Missouri: Your love and support pushes me onward every day. I love all of y'all.

Willetta Harmon: Just for EVERYTHING. Especially the food, Sistah Willetta.

Billy Masters: If your talented ass sends me one more puzzle it's gon' be your ass. Thank you for the constant laughter.

Ryan Raftery: I don't know how a little white boy worked his way into my life, but I'm sho'nuff glad he did. If you wake me up again singing those loud-ass, funny-ass songs . . . you know the rest. So proud of you.

Brian Norbert: The man with the mildew pants. I hated you then, I hate you still. Thank you for your artistry on all fronts. I want to take this time to apologize for fucking up your back during the Duke of Earl at Six Flags Over Mid-America when we were both seventeen years old. I love you.

Queen Latifah: For driving me home when I was drunk.

Gail Lerner: Your *courage* and *strength* taught me to love life more. Thank you for allowing me to dedicate my book to your children.

Dr. Sears: For the bipolar medication. Y'all should bow down to this mothaFucka.

My siblings: Jackie, Robin, Larry, Vertrella, Wilatrel. I love you so much.

Tammy Ader: Thank you for the TV series *Strong Medicine* and your enormous heart.

Ezekiel Davis: My dear brother-in-law, RIP.

Julia Walker: Thank you for taking that first cold dip and becoming a wolf. Thank you for absolutely everything.

LaWanda Smith: The first time I saw you, you were laughing. When I was having a hard time, you came to my door laughing. We've been laughing ever since. Thank you for your professionalism, loyalty, and trust. Thank you for not really charging me the pain-in-the-ass fee.

Michelle Cole: We have the same soul. The same hopes and dreams. We're the same age, but you look younger. I won't curse you out 'cause I love you too much. Thank you for making me pretty on *black-ish*. I love you, Michelle.

Stanley Hudson: You made me laugh, you made me pretty, and I love you for it. Thank you.

All my babies on the *black-ish* crew: I can't name you all, but you know who you are. I miss you so much even from afar. You put up with my shit for eight wonderful years. Goodbye-*ish black-ish*. I'm over here in tears. I love you all and Godspeed.

Yossef Aviv: You built me a home. It's so special to me. I love you, Yossef. And I know you love me. Thank you. For EVERYTHING.

Maxine Waters: The world thanks you. I thank you, and Kinloch thanks you. Lotsa love to my OG home gurl.

Dr. Neal ElAttrache: Thank you for fixing both my shoulders and my right knee. You've been so very good to me. Thank you, Dr. ElAttrache.

Roma Little-Walker: We met in the Sahara Desert back in the day. I love our friendship. Every day.

Dokhi Mirmirani at Jasmine Blue Flowers: You explode my soul every time I hear your voice. Your flowers have made my house a home.

Mark Sendroff: Thank you for always being there for me. I love you deeply.

Jeffrey Gunter: I loved you in the beginning. I'll love you in the end. Thanks for taking amazing care of me, Jeffrey.

Sam Haskell: My first agent in Hollywood. Thank you for loving me so damn much. Give Mary and Mary a big kiss.

Keith L. Alexander: Oh dear God, what can I say about my baby? Just thank you for always being there, Keith. All the great conversations, the booming laughter, and helping me see the light at the end of the tunnel.

Mario: The one man I can depend on to laugh at any and every gotdamn thing I say. I love you and Aaron to the moon.

Steven White: I know you're white, but you're Black to me. Big kiss.

Kevin Reher: You gave me Mama Odie and Flo. I'm glad you know good Black don't crack. I love you, Kevin.

Deborah Dean Davis: Not a day goes by I don't think of you with a smile. You're an amazing writer. Thank you for pushing me to continue writing.

Iona Morris: For eight years you helped me with my lines on *black-ish* and lived to tell the story. I love you. Let's do a hot tub soon.

Dr. Elizabeth Stroebel: President of Webster University. Thank you for my honorary doctorate and trusting me to send eleven thousand of your graduates out into the world.

Linda Saputo: Since college, when you walked into the dressing room and saw how I applied my lipstick. The shock and laughter has never ceased. My love for you is slightly stupid. Now sing it with me: "Have a good day. I want you to be my friend."

Valente Frazier: Hello, Peaches. Why don't you stop laughing so damn hard when you do my makeup? Thank you for making me so pretty. Track 1: mothaFucka.

Niecy Nash: When you imitated me on Halloween, all I could do was scream. I love your beautiful, talented ass.

Roz Ryan: My ride-or-die gangsta. Thanks for looking out and being a loving big sister. Happy whale watching.

Annette Lewis: I don't know anybody in the world sweeter than you. I just don't.

Brian Edwards: Thank you for you. The fun, the fun, the laughter, the fun. This is the man who is mostly responsible for me receiving my star on the Hollywood Walk of Fame. Bow down, bitches.

Career Overview

(Listed in alphabetical order)

Broadway*

Comin' Uptown, 1979–1980

Eubie!, 1978–1979

Hairspray, 2008

Rock 'N Roll! The First 5,000 Years, 1982

Feature Films and Animation†

Antwone Fisher, "Aunt" (uncredited), 2002

Baggage Claim, "Catherine," 2013

Beaches, "Diva," 1988

Blast from the Past, "Dr. Aron," 1999

---

*   More information at ibdb.com

†   More information at imdb.com

The Brothers, "Louise Smith," 2001

Cars, "Flo" (voice), 2006

Cars 2, "Flo" (voice), 2011

Cars 3, "Flo" (voice), 2017

Cast Away, "Becca Twig," 2000

The Cookout, "Lady Em," 2004

Corrina, Corrina, "Jevina," 1994

Dancing in September, "Judge Warner," 2000

Dead Presidents, "Mrs. Curtis," 1995

Dirty Laundry, "Aunt Lettuce," 2006

The Exes, "Caren Dupree," 2015

Frozen Assets, "Jomisha," 1992

Girl 6, "Boss #1—Lil," 1996

The Heart Specialist, "Nurse Jackson," 2006

Hereafter, "Candace," 2010

Juwanna Mann, "Aunt Ruby," 2002

Madea's Family Reunion, "Milay Jenay Lori," 2006

Meet the Browns, "Vera," 2008

The Meteor Man, "Mrs. Williams, Lewis's Mother," 1993

The Mighty, "Mrs. Addison," 1998

Mystery Men, "Lucille," 1999

Nora's Hair Salon, "Nora Harper," 2004

Not Easily Broken, "Mary 'Mama' Clark," 2009

Panther, "Rita," 1995

Playin' for Love, "Alize Gates," 2013

Poetic Justice, "Annie," 1993

The Preacher's Wife, "Margueritte Coleman," 1996

The Princess and the Frog, "Mama Odie" (voice), 2009

Prop 8: The Musical, "Riffing Prop 8'er," Film Short, 2008

Red Heat, "Judge Jenifer Lewis" (uncredited), 1988

Redrum, "Therapist," 2007

Renaissance Man, "Mrs. Coleman," 1994

Rituals, Film Short, 1998

Secrets of the Magic City, "Aunt Valerie," 2014

Shark Tale, "Motown Turtle" (voice), 2004

Sister Act, "Michelle," 1992

Sister Act 2: Back in the Habit, "Vegas Backup Singer #1," 1993

The Sunday Morning Stripper, "Demetria," Film Short, 2003

Think Like a Man, "Loretta," 2012

Think Like a Man Too, "Loretta," 2014

Undercover Blues, "Cab Driver," 1993

The Wedding Ringer, "Doris Jenkins," 2015

What's Love Got to Do with It, "Zelma Bullock," 1993

When Harry Met Sally 2 with Billy Crystal and Helen Mirren, "Retirement Home Waitress," Video short, 2011

Who's Your Caddy?, "C-Note's Mom," 2007

Zambezia, "Gogo," 2012

Television*

American Dad!, "Lessie" (voice), 1 episode, 2011

An Unexpected Life, "Camile," TV Movie, 1998

Bette, "Inez," 1 episode, 2000

Big Hero 6: The Series, "Professor Granville," 2 episodes, 2017

black-ish, "Ruby," 56 episodes, 2014–

The Boondocks, "Geraldine/Boss Willona" (voice), 2014

Boston Legal, "Judge Isabel Fisher," 2 episodes, 2007–2008

The Cleveland Show, "Receptionist/Middle-Aged Woman/Woman/ Kevin Garnett's Mom" (voice), 2 episodes, 2011

Cosby, "Bernice," 1 episode, 1996

Courthouse, "Judge Rosetta Reide," 11 episodes, 1995

Day Break, "Elizabeth Hopper," 1 episode, 2007

Deadline for Murder: From the Files of Edna Buchanan, "Denice Cooper," TV Movie, 1995

---

* More information at imdb.com

Deconstructing Sarah, "Betty," TV Movie, 1994

A Different World, "Susan Clayton/Dean Dorothy Dandridge Davenport," 9 episodes, 1990–1993

Dream On, "Carolyn," 1 episode, 1992

Elena of Avalor, "Tornado," 1 episode, 2017

Family Affair, "Mrs. Summers," pilot episode, 2002

Five, "Maggie," TV Movie, 2011

For Your Love, "Mel and Reggie's Mother/Sylvia Ellis," 2 episodes, 1998–2000

The Fresh Prince of Bel-Air, "Aunt Helen," 8 episodes, 1991–1996

Friends, "Paula," 1 episode, 1994

Girlfriends, "Veretta Childs," 7 episodes, 2002–2006

Grown-ups, "Melissa's Mother," 1 episode, 1999

Hangin' with Mr. Cooper, "Georgia Rodman," 2 episodes, 1992–1994

Happily Ever After: Fairy Tales for Every Child, "Hazel/Black Widow Spider" (voice), 2 episodes, 1997–1999

In Living Color, various, 2 episodes, 1993

Instant Mom, "Delois," 2 episodes, 2015

It Had to Be You, "Reggie," TV Movie, 2015

Jackie's Back!, "Jackie Washington," TV Movie, 1999

The Jamie Foxx Show, "Josie," 1 episode, 1999

Last Days of Russell, "Aunt Yvette," TV Movie, 1994

Little Richard, "Muh Penniman," TV Movie, 2000

Living Single, "Delia Deveaux," 1 episode, 1995

Lois & Clark: The New Adventures of Superman, "Mystique," 1 episode, 1994

Meet the Browns, "Vera Brown," 5 episodes, 2009–2010

Moesha, "Mrs. Biggs," 1 episode, 1999

Moon Over Miami, "Aurora Tyler," 1 episode, 1993

Murphy Brown, "Sales Person," 2 episodes, 1990–1991

New York Undercover, "Medina," 1 episode, 1995

The Parent 'Hood, "Linda," 1998

Partners, "Detective Lancy," TV Movie, 2000

Piper's Picks TV, "Herself," 1 episode, 2012

The PJs, "Bebe Ho," 36 episodes, 1999–2001

The Playboy Club, "Pearl," 7 episodes, 2011

The Ponder Heart, "Narcissa Wingfield," TV Movie, 2001

Promised Land, "Queenie," 1 episode, 1997

The Proud Family, 2001–2005, "Aunt Spice" (voice), 1 episode, 2003

Rebel Highway, "Amanda Baldwin Cooper," 1 episode, 1994

Roc, "Charlaine," 1 episode, 1993

Shark, "Ellie Broussard," 1 episode, 2007

Shattle, Rattle and Rock!, "Amanda," TV Movie, 1994

Stat, "Felicia Brown," 1 episode, 1991

State of Georgia, "Patrice," 1 episode, 2011

Strong Medicine, "Lana Hawkins," 131 episodes, 2000– 2006

Sunday in Paris, "Taylor Chase," TV Short, 1991

Tales from Radiator Springs, "Flo" (voice), 2 episodes, 2013–2014

The Temptations, "Mama Rose," 2 episodes, 1998

That's So Raven, "Vivian Baxter," 1 episode, 2004

Time of Your Life, "Joss's Mother," 1 episode, 1999

Touched by an Angel, "Queenie," 1 episode, 1997

Young Justice, "Olympia," 1 episode, 2017

Video Games** (Voices)

Cars, "Flo," 2006

Cars 2: The Video Game, "Flo," 2011

Cars Mater-National, "Flo," 2007

Cars Race-O-Rama, "Flo," 2009

Disney Infinity, "Flo," 2013

The Princess and the Frog, "Mama Odie," 2009

Sorcerers of the Magic Kingdom, "Mama Odie/Shenzi," 2012

---

*   More information at imdb.com

Social Media Videos

Amazing Grace. YouTube. Marc Shaiman. May 31, 2017

An Artist's Duty (aka 50 Million of Us), with Brandy and Roz Ryan. Instagram. jeniferlewisforreal, January 16, 2017.

Brandy, Roz Ryan, & Jenifer Lewis Perform "In These Streets." YouTube. ForeverBrandy. May 6, 2016. Retrieved from https://youtu.be/Ud2E6TSfJ0M

How You Gonna Call SOMEONE ELSE #Legend, with Brandy and Todrick Hall. Instagram. jeniferlewisforreal. October 6, 2016.

Jenifer Lewis—Carnegie Hall "Shaiman/Wittman" Tribute—"I Know Where I've Been." YouTube. Shangela L. Wadley. April 29, 2014.

Jenifer Lewis and Marc Shaiman Preview "Black Don't Crack" and More! playbill.com.

Jenifer Lewis and Shangela: Ep. 1: Doo Doo. YouTube. Jenifer Lewis and Shangela. September 4, 2012.

Jenifer Lewis and Shangela: Ep. 2: Recognition. YouTube. Jenifer Lewis and Shangela. September 12, 2012.

Jenifer Lewis and Shangela: Ep. 3: Gold Earring. Jenifer Lewis and Shangela. September 18, 2012.

Jenifer Lewis and Shangela: Ep. 4: Mouse. Jenifer Lewis and Shangela. September 25, 2012.

Jenifer Lewis Performs Last Dance at APLA Commitment to Life Event. TheJeniferLewis. June 21, 2011.

Jenifer Lewis Gives Powerful Speech at Baggage Claim Premiere. YouTube. TrueExclusives. September 20, 2013

Jenifer Lewis Gives Webster University Commencement Speech. YouTube. Webster University. May 12, 2015

Jenifer Lewis' Get Your Ass Out and Vote. YouTube. TheJeniferLewis. November 8, 2016.

Jenifer Lewis on Oprah. YouTube. TheJeniferLewis. May 8, 2011.

Josh Gad Impersonates Jenifer Lewis on the set of The Wedding Ringer. YouTube. Sony Pictures Entertainment. January 14, 2015.

"Pussy Bone." YouTube. Marc Shaiman. May 23, 2017.

Social Media Handles

Facebook: http://www.facebook.com/JeniferLewisForReal

Instagram: www.instagram.com/jeniferlewisforreal/

Twitter: @jeniferlewis

About the Author

Dubbed a national treasure and a force to be reckoned with, award-winning actress Jenifer Lewis starred on ABC's *black-ish* as the hilarious grandmother Ruby Johnson, which earned her a nomination for the 2016 Critics' Choice Award. She has appeared in over four hundred episodic television shows, sixty-eight movies, forty animations, and four Broadway productions, such as *The Fresh Prince of Bel-Air*; *Friends*; *A Different World*; *Twenties*; *Cast Away*; *What's Love Got to Do with It*; *Think Like a Man*; *Madea's Family Reunion*; *Strong Medicine*; *The Princess and the Frog*; *Mickey Mouse Funhouse*; *Rugrats*; *Cars 1, 2,* and *3*; *American Dad!*; and *Hairspray*. She has performed in more than two hundred concerts worldwide, including to sold-out audiences at Lincoln Center and garnering an electrifying standing ovation at Carnegie Hall. Her accomplishments as an entertainer, community activist, and author have been recognized with an honorary doctorate from her alma mater, Webster University, and the Career Achievement Award from the American Black Film Festival. In 2022, Ms. Lewis stars in a new television series, *I Love That for You*, on Showtime. She will also receive her star on the Hollywood Walk of Fame on July 15, 2022 (on Jackie Washington Day). She was born and raised in Kinloch, Missouri, and lives in Los Angeles with her bichon frise, Butters Lewis.